"This is **the kind of no-nonsense book with practical advice that every newcomer to the arena of raising money should read.** As an investment banker, I could save myself thousands of hours and companies thousands of dollars if they would each read this book."

> STEVE PUTNAM
> President, Robert Thomas Securities
> Former Chairman, National Association of
> Securities Dealers, Inc.
> Former Chairman, Boston Stock Exchange

"*Where to Go When the Bank Says No* is **more than a 'how to' guide for entrepreneurs**, it doubles as a resource directory with **an abundance of contact information.**"

> RICH BENDIS
> President
> Kansas Technology Enterprise Corp.

"Given the tremendous contribution small business makes to the U.S. economy in terms of jobs and innovation, **it's about time someone told small-business people where to go and what to do when they get there.** *Where to Go When the Bank Says No* is **a tightly written manual** on the how, where, what, and why of small-business finance. **It ought to be the most well-thumbed book in every businessperson's collection.**"

> TOM STEWART-GORDON
> Editor
> *SCOR Report*

Where TO Go WHEN THE Bank Says No

BLOOMBERG SMALL BUSINESS

David R. Evanson

Where TO Go WHEN THE Bank Says No

**ALTERNATIVES
FOR FINANCING
YOUR BUSINESS**

BLOOMBERG PRESS

PRINCETON

Books are available for bulk purchases at special discounts. Special editions or book excerpts can also be created to specifications. For information, please write: Special Markets Department, Bloomberg Press.

This publication contains the author's opinions and is designed to provide accurate and authoritative information. It is sold with the understanding that the author, publisher, and Bloomberg L.P. are not engaged in rendering legal, accounting, investment-planning, or other professional advice. The reader should seek the services of a qualified professional for such advice; the author, publisher, and Bloomberg L.P. cannot be held responsible for any loss incurred as a result of specific investments or planning decisions made by the reader.

First edition published 1998

3 5 7 9 10 8 6 4 2

Evanson, David R.
    Where to go when the bank says no: alternatives for financing your business / David R. Evanson. - - 1st ed.
        p.   cm.
    Includes index.
        ISBN 1-57660-017-3 (alk. paper)
        1. New business enterprises - -United States - -Finance. 2. Venture capital - -United States. 3. Small business - -United States- - Finance.
I. Title.
HG4027.6.E89   1998
658. 15'224- -dc21   98-9682
                                                                  CIP

ACQUIRED AND EDITED BY
Steven Gittelson

BOOK DESIGN BY
Don Morris Design

*This book is
dedicated to Perri, and to
Madeline and David.*

ACKNOWLEDGMENTS

LIKE RAISING CAPITAL, A PROJECT SUCH AS THIS BOOK OWES its completion, and hopefully its success, to many other people.

I'd like to thank Greg Matusky, a partner but also a brilliant writer and public relations professional, who taught me the power of telling a good story. Steve Glazer always kept my finger on the pulse of the Internet, in terms of its capital-formation potential. Likewise, Drew Field, one of the country's foremost authorities on direct public offerings, helped me explain some of the extremely complex legal issues in straightforward prose, something that the Securities and Exchange Commission has yet to accomplish. Paul Rosenbaum, one of the country's first true venture capitalists, provided invaluable insight on stalking angel investors, along with Miles Spencer from *Money Hunt*. Likewise, Jeffrey Sohl at the University of New Hampshire, Rich Bendis at the Kansas Technology Enterprise Corporation, Bard Salmon at the Technology Capital Network, and William Wetzel, professor emeritus at the University of New Hampshire, all architects in one way or another of the current public policy on angel investors, shared their deep well of knowledge with me.

I owe the editors of *Entrepreneur* magazine, including Editorial Director Rieva Lesonsky, as well as Maria Anton, Maria Valdez, Peggy Bennett, and Karen Axelton, a deep debt of gratitude for publishing my column "Raising Money" each month and giving me the freedom to explore this topic all the way to the fringes.

Many investors contributed to this project as well. Some of these include John Martinson at Edison Ventures; Fred Beste at NEPA Venture Funds; Ric Klass of M.S. Farrell; members of the Loosely Organized Retired Executives; Art Beroff; Herbert Cohen; Ron Conway of the Band of Angels; Steve Hope; David Freschman of the Delaware Innovation Fund; David Menard; Ted Schlein of Kleiner, Perkins, Caufield & Byers; John Lane of Westport Resources Investment Corporation; Ben Lichtenberg at First Colonial Securities; Peter Ligeti at Keystone Venture Capital; Tony Petrelli of Neidiger/Tucker/Bruner, and Jim Twaddell with Schneider Securities.

Two investors who took a big risk early on include Greame Howard and Jes Lawson. Thank you.

There are also several entrepreneurs who deserve credit for reminding me what life is like in the trenches and whose stories pepper this work. These include Gerry Powell at Cooperative Images; Chuck Torrey at Energy Search; Zindel Zelmanovitch at Freshstart Venture Capital; Gary Veloric, Jim Delaney, and Michael Goodman at J. G. Wentworth; Ed Meltzer at Intelligent Wireless Systems; Rick Ill and John Bartholdson of the Triumph Group; Bill Spane and Larry Donato of BHC Financial; Rod Vahle of Accent on Animals; Darius and Bill Bikoff of Energy Brands, Inc.; Bob Ginsburg and Alan Goldberg at Marlton Technologies, and Jim Young.

Dean Schwartz at Stradley, Ronan, Stevens & Young; Jeff Aducci of Regional Investment Bankers; Steve Putnam of Robert Thomas Securities; Philip Webster of The Webster Group; Lee Marshall of BusinessWire; Roger Thompson of *Nation's Business;* and Barry Suskind of International Technologies & Finance provided input, direction, and the support required to make this project a possibility. Also, thank you to Stanley Evanson, my father, who grew a successful business without raising any money.

I would also like to thank Nancy Scarlato and Jim Sullivan, who kept Financial Communications Associates functioning in top form while this project was being completed, and for their diligent research throughout the process.

Finally, thank you to Bloomberg, including Michael Bloomberg, the font of it all; Jared Kieling, who said yes; and Steven Gittelson, who kept a steady hand on the tiller and always had an encouraging word. Thanks, too, to Stephen Solomon for his organizing ideas.

As you can see, this book owes its good points to many investors, entrepreneurs, writers, editors, and business people. Its flaws, on the other hand, have been furnished exclusively by me.

Introduction

THIS BOOK IS WRITTEN FOR ENTREPRENEURS WITH
small or new businesses who need to raise between
$250,000 and $15 million. However, knowing
where to look for capital is only one of the ingre-
dients required for success. If this were not the case,
a financing directory and a telephone would be all
you would need.

Unfortunately, many entrepreneurs fail in their
search for capital because they are unprepared to
raise capital, and they approach the wrong investors. This book gives you valuable insights in both
areas: where and how to look for equity capital.

The first section is the one that gave the book its
title—*Where to Go When the Bank Says No*. The
first chapter explores why debt is not the proper
source of financing for emerging growth
companies. From my experience talking with
thousands of entrepreneurs looking for capital, I've
learned that many do not understand why banks will

2

not lend them money. Worse, others are not aware of the serious drawbacks of debt financing.

The next four chapters discuss the primary sources of equity capital. These are angels, initial public offerings, alternative routes to a public offering, and venture capital. Each of these chapters explains not only how to find these investors, but also the sizes and shapes of the companies that interest them. Chapter 6 explores less-visible means of financing your company, such as the use of incubators, royalty financing, community loan development funds, and even your own 401(k) plan.

The second section of this book, Chapters 7 through 9, discusses financial analysis, valuation, and business plans. The purpose of these chapters is to help entrepreneurs prepare themselves to make the best possible presentation to equity investors.

The first two appendices contain valuable contacts that can lead you to equity capital. Appendix A contains a detailed listing of venture capital clubs and networks by region. Appendix B lists the top university-based entrepreneurial programs that offer a path to angel investors. One of the underlying themes of this book is that raising capital requires making connections with other people. These two directories show you a way to take the first step easily and painlessly. Finally, Appendix C offers a summary of some of the securities laws that may affect your deal; read it so that you'll know what your lawyer and accountant are talking about.

This book covers a lot of ground in very few pages, a feat that is at once satisfying and a little bit frightening. This brevity is based on my trust in the ability of entrepreneurs to grasp concepts quickly and to recognize that raising money is a lot like selling their own products and services. If the readers of this book are anything like the many entrepreneurs I have met or any of the now-famous ones who have changed our landscape forever, I'm certain this trust is well founded.

DAVID R. EVANSON

Sources
of Equity
Capital

CHAPTER 1

Focusing on Equity Capital

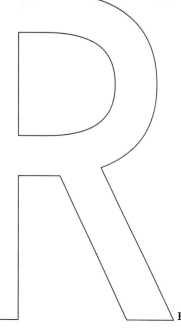EST ASSURED, THE BANK WILL SAY
no. But a bank is not the right place for a small
company to obtain capital for growth, anyway. If you
want to understand why this is so, visit the lobby of
your local bank. There you will see some people
putting money in the bank, and others taking it out
again. People asking the tellers for cash have every
expectation that their money will be available when
they need it.

And that, in a nutshell, is the problem.

The bank can't lend your fledgling business the
money it needs for growth because that's not the
deal it has made with depositors. Money is
deposited with the understanding that nothing too
exotic is going to be done with it. After all, it's a
deposit—not a contribution to a hedge fund,
venture capital partnership, or buyout group. In fact,
if you're a real purist, a deposit is itself a *loan* to the

bank. If someone lent *you* funds that had to be repaid immediately upon demand, would you then lend the money to a company that was developing a product but had no sales?

This arrangement leads bankers down a very narrow and predictable path. They can only make loans in situations in which the money is safe and repayment is almost certain. So, who qualifies for such a loan from a bank? Established companies may qualify if they can repay the loan from cash flow, and if that dries up, then from the liquidation of assets. Even if a company has the assets, or collateral, to cover a loan, it still might not be worth the risk. After all, if the deal goes south, the bank has to sell the assets to get its money back. These assets might not fetch as much as the bank thinks. Or they may be difficult to sell at all. Suddenly, the bank starts paying carrying costs and the whole situation quickly gets messy. Banks, therefore, only want to lend to customers who can pay them back easily.

These facts notwithstanding, untold numbers of entrepreneurs go knocking on the door of their local banks looking for capital. When a banker hears the words "cutting-edge Internet business" roll off the tongue of a loan seeker, the banker's eyes start to glaze; she might start thinking, "How do I get out of this gracefully?" As she goes through her routine set of questions for the entrepreneur, the banker is probably imagining her own unspoken replies:

Is the product or service complete, or does the company need funding to develop it?

We don't fund research and development, because there is no source of repayment associated with it.

If the R&D was funded, could the product be successfully developed?

Even if we did fund product development, which we don't, I don't think that what would be left, in terms of a patent or equipment, would be worth nearly the loan value. The last time we tried to sell the rights we had to technology, it was a disaster.

Are there any assets or inventory here to collateralize the loan?

By the time we enforce our lien, their Pentium desktops will be paperweights and doorstops.

If it's a new product or service, will the market buy it?

Hmmm, I don't know a single person with an Apple Newton. And it's not just technology that flops. The other day I asked for New Coke with my Big Mac and learned that they don't make New Coke anymore.

Will customers pay for the product or service? What percentage of sales will be bad debts?

It makes me nervous when there is not an established pool of buyers with a payment history. Plus, if the service or product is unproven, will buyers withhold payment until it works according to their expectations?

Will this company grow too fast for its own good?

Our rate of return has no bearing on how fast the company grows. If it grows too fast, we may even have to write off the entire loan because the company crashes and burns.

The Government Can't Help You

WHEN ENTREPRENEURS COME FACE-TO-FACE WITH THE FACT
that they can't get a bank loan, many of them turn to the federal government's Small Business Administration (SBA). This can be a good idea. However, it can also be a bad idea if entrepreneurs believe they have an inalienable right to a loan. The concept of "entitlements," which carries significant currency in the federal government, has no value at the SBA.

Regarding small-business finance, the SBA is mostly about guaranteeing bank loans. Its cornerstone effort is the 7(a) loan guarantee program, which guarantees up to $750,000 of a private-sector loan. The reasoning goes that if a bank sees a guarantee on as much as 75 percent of the principal (in some cases, 80 percent), it will make loans that otherwise would be too risky. However, SBA-guaranteed loans aren't subsidized, low-rate loans. Rates are competitive, but capped at no more than the prime rate plus 2.75 percent.

While the 7(a) program helps many companies, it's not a panacea for small business. Why? When deciding whether or not to issue a guarantee for a loan, the SBA conducts exactly the same credit analysis that a banking officer does. According to Michael Dowd, director of the SBA's Office of Loan Programs, the agency actually turns down guarantees on some loans that banks have already approved.

No matter what the sources of the money, emerging businesses will never truly emerge if they are financed with debt. A company cannot grow unless it's able to plow all of its cash flow back into the business. Diverting cash from the business in the form of monthly principal and interest payments can be debilitating—even when the rate of interest is well below the margins that a company earns.

Consider for a moment a secured loan for $300,000 with a five-year term and 12 percent annual interest for a financial-services company. The monthly nut for the loan is $6,700. However, since the lender will need comfort above and beyond $6,700, he or she may require covenants in the loan that the company maintain an average cash flow of 125 percent of the interest payments, or in this case, some

Good example of the cost of capital.

$8,375. That is, the company must have an average of $8,375 left over every month when it subtracts monthly operating expenses from monthly revenues to pay the $6,700 in principal and interest payments.

Financial services firms like the one in this example, with annual sales between $1 million and $3 million, have an average net operating margin of 7 percent, according to Robert Morris Associates, a banking trade group in Philadelphia that produces financial-statement studies so lenders can understand industry norms for financial performance. Assuming operating income equals cash flow, how much business must the company do on a monthly basis just to break even after debt service? The answer: $96,000. And what annual revenue must the company generate to ensure that it's maintaining the net cash flow the bank requires? This time: $1.7 million. For unsecured loans—those guaranteed by the borrower, rather than collateralized by underlying assets—the hurdles will be even higher.

The hill is steep, indeed, for companies financed with debt. The $300,000 loan proceeds must generate nearly six times their value just to keep the bank happy. They must generate about four times their value for the company to break even. The situation would be even bleaker if the new business happened to be a bookbinding manufacturer instead of a commercial finance company. With average net operating margins of only 2.3 percent, according to studies prepared by Robert Morris Associates, the company would have to generate $3.5 million from the loan proceeds to break even after paying interest.

There's no doubt that savvy executives can turn $300,000 of capital, even debt capital, into $3 million, or perhaps even $300 million, given one essential ingredient: *time*. However, in the same way that sources and uses of funds can sometimes get mismatched, so, too, can the sources and uses of time. Unfortunately, banks provide emerging companies a limited amount of time—certainly not as much as it takes to grow the business.

Advertising agencies generate a lot of marketing juice by suggesting that businesses move at the speed of light. Some do. However, most companies move at the speed of cold tar. For many, the sales cycle takes months and months.

It's not hard to see why. Small-business owners have to wait it out as a Fortune 500 company spends six months trying to figure out if it wants to test database marketing through an outside vendor, and another six months trying to get the project budgeted. Or a retailer waits four months for a site to open up and then spends three months on leasehold improvements. And so it goes.

All this waiting is at odds with the demands of a commercial loan. The loan payment is due every month or every quarter; new business gets booked at a more random pace.

Another reason debt financing is inappropriate for growth companies is because it's not permanent. It has to be paid back, and sometimes payment comes due at an inopportune time. A missed loan payment may cause the lender to force repayment when the company is not ready to do so. Or the bank may decide to shift its market focus, declaring it is no longer interested in some of its commercial customers.

According to borrower's-rights attorney Barry Cappello, of the Santa Barbara law firm Cappello & McCann, small-business borrowers occupy a precarious position as the banking industry consolidates through acquisitions. Cappello says that when one bank acquires another, the borrower faces two possible and unpleasant side effects. First, new management may decide that the bank is no longer interested in particular industries or in loans below a certain size. Second, new owners often bring in new loan officers as well, with each new officer trying to ratchet up the terms of the loan.

One anonymous Cappello client, who is suing his bank over the termination of a line of credit, reported that during his 10-year relationship there were seven different branch managers, eight commercial loan officers, two regional vice presidents, and four assistant regional vice presidents. "It's scary," he says. "Here's an institution that holds the destiny of your company in its hand, that has a lien on all of your corporate and personal assets, and every time you walk in there's a different person who wants to play by a new set of rules."

One company that suffered from the impermanence of a bank loan was Capehart Electronics. Ed Culverwell, an investment banker with Culverwell & Company in Boston, remembers it well, since it resulted in perhaps one of the most amazing deals in his lifetime.

The tale dates back to 1927, when salesman Homer E. Capehart started his company. So aggressive and relentless was Capehart that *Fortune* magazine was compelled to write of him in 1941: "One of the highest powered, highest pressure salesmen this country has ever produced." However, Capehart's drive paid off. His name became synonymous with sound quality and high fidelity, long after he became a U.S. senator in 1944.

The Capehart name was still intact during the early 1970s. In fact, demographics may have given it even more cachet. As baby boomers reached their teenage years, they clamored for stereo equipment. Their parents, shopping among the

Orientation Comparisons

LENDER ORIENTATION

Wants to see plenty of hard assets on the balance sheet to collateralize a loan.

Isn't concerned with intangibles such as trademarks, copyrights, and goodwill, which have no liquidation value.

Doesn't care about other liabilities; gets paid off first in a liquidation.

Frightened by meteoric growth because it can destabilize a company.

Prefers to finance companies that will need additional debt as they grow.

Favors big loans.

Likes proven markets with proven receivables.

Wants to structure deals so that the company or its founders pay back what they borrowed.

Liquidates companies in order to get money back.

foreign-looking gadgetry on the shelves of "hi-fi" stores, immediately identified with the name Capehart.

Recognizing this, the late entrepreneur and businessman Leonard Kaye bought the rights to the name and began selling Capehart stereos through Zayres and other discount department store chains. Culverwell underwrote a $1 million equity offering in 1971 to help finance the company. Sales mushroomed from $4 million to $12 million the next year. The stock soared from $5 to $30, recalls Culverwell. Demand was scalding hot, and in anticipation of hitting $60 million in sales during 1974, Capehart bulked up on bank-financed inventory.

Then interest rates took off. The prime rate hit 12 percent, two points higher than Capehart's 10 percent margin. As rates increased, sales slowed because consumers were less willing to purchase major appliances on credit. The company's bank got nervous, says Culverwell. "They took posses-

EQUITY INVESTOR ORIENTATION

Doesn't care about hard assets. Probably won't see a dime if the company ever liquidates.

Favors intangible assets, which represent a competitive edge that can drive sales.

Concerned about liabilities; wants capital to build the business, not bail out creditors.

Wants to see meteoric growth.

Likes companies with operating leverage because it increases profitability.

Careful to avoid companies that will outrun the capital they're prepared to provide.

Likes proven markets, too, but also attracted to new markets in which there is an opportunity to establish a dominant position.

Structures deals so that other equity investors will later buy them out at a premium.

Tries to save companies in order to get investment back.

sion of the inventory and liquidated it at bargain basement prices to pay off the company's line," he says. Suddenly, high-flying Capehart Electronics was out of business.

A Better Strategy

BECAUSE BANK LOANS ARE USUALLY A POOR CHOICE FOR growing companies, often the better strategy is to look for equity financing. An equity investor puts capital into a company and gets stock—part ownership—back in return. The equity investor doesn't receive interest payments; the financing is *permanent*. Instead, an investor shares in the increasing *value* of the company.

Consider the preceding differences in the orientation of a lender and an equity investor. Note how the equity investor's focus matches an entrepreneur's, while the lender's focus tends to be at odds with that of the business owner.

CHAPTER 2

Securing Capital from Angels

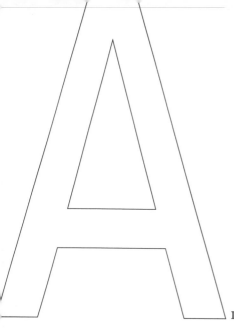

LTHOUGH EQUITY FINANCING is the proper mode of financing for any growing business, it comes in different forms. Entrepreneurs must decide what type of equity is right for their business.

Broadly speaking, venture capital is a generic term that describes any capital invested in risky, young companies. Sources of venture capital include angels, who are wealthy individual investors working alone or in loose confederacies; professional venture capital firms, which are partnerships that manage and invest a pool of money and are often quite large; and public venture capital, which is raised through stock sales to the public, called initial public offerings, or IPOs.

For most businesses, equity capital from angels is the optimal form of financing. Why?

◆ Capital from angels is the most abundant source of

capital available.

- ◆ The amount of capital sought for early-stage businesses, typically $250,000 to $5 million, matches the commitments that angels typically make.
- ◆ Angels also can provide the kind of assistance in strategic planning and other business issues that growing companies typically need.

Angels are everywhere. Jeffrey Sohl, director of the Center for Venture Research at the University of New Hampshire, estimates that there are 250,000 angels in the United States. Each year, Sohl says, these angels invest $20 billion to $30 billion in approximately 30,000 growing businesses. This figure, incidentally, dwarfs the $5 billion to $7 billion invested each year by institutional venture capitalists.

To get angels to invest in your business, you must meet with them because your deal will be consummated on personal chemistry and economics.

To meet angels you must first generate leads. Before you generate leads, you must first write a business plan *(see Chapter 9)* because investors must look it over before they will agree to meet. Overall, raising capital from angels requires planning. Assuming you've written a business plan, here's how to find and get capital from angel investors.

Where to Find Angels

ANGELS TEND TO HOVER AROUND EASILY IDENTIFIED, AND IN many cases, easily accessed centers of activity. Listed below are some places to go to find them and start generating leads. You can find detailed lists of specific sources in Appendices A and B.

◆ **Venture capital forums.** "Venture capital forum" is a general term, referring to the financing, education, and networking opportunities that are sponsored by chambers of commerce, economic development coalitions, publishers, and professional services organizations such as law and accounting firms. Attend meetings in your area and ask people there for the names of investors you can contact. Fees for entrepreneurs are nominal, typically $15 to $50.

For instance, the MIT Enterprise Forum®, Inc. now operates in 14 cities in the United States. In these forums, a panel of professional venture capitalists who have read a business plan several days in advance evaluate the company and the deal, in front of the entrepreneur. There are audience participation, feedback, and questions and answers.

◆ **Venture capital clubs.** So-called clubs or consortiums are groups of individual private investors who meet on a regular basis to hear formal presentations from entrepreneurs seeking capital. For the most part, these investors own a business and are eager to invest in others.

Typically, clubs solicit business plans that are reviewed by a screening committee that frequently is affiliated with a university or economic development council. The review committee selects certain plans and invites the entrepreneur-authors to spend between 10 and 30 minutes making a formal presentation before the club's members. Interested club members follow up on their own. While members tend to invest independently, they sometimes team up on deals, as well.

The screening committee may or may not select your company for a formal presentation before the club. *Even if you are rejected, the people who reviewed your plan can point you toward other investors.*

◆ **Private capital networks.** Networks are essentially electronic matching services that put entrepreneurs and angels together, based upon a similarity of needs and preferences. Almost all networks have a university or economic development council affiliation.

Private capital networks work best with face-to-face networking and educational programs for both entrepreneurs and investors. According to Peter Bechtel, who runs the North Carolina Investor Network, an electronic matching service affiliated with the North Carolina Small Business and Technology Development Center, a definite correlation exists between these kinds of activities and investment commitments.

Angels register with a network and provide detailed information about their investment preferences on items such as industries or technologies, minimum- and maximum-deal sizes, geographic restrictions, willingness to coinvest with other investors, stage of development, and level of hands-on involvement in the company. The networks, which are regional, usually enroll 100 to 500 angels interested in seeing business proposals.

Entrepreneurs pay a fee, typically $100 to $500, to register with the network and provide a detailed summary of their company and financing needs, as well as the executive summary of their business plan. A computer matches companies with investors in the network, based upon their shared interests and characteristics.

The network administrator sends to the selected angels an executive summary of the company's business plan and the name of the entrepreneur. Some networks also send the entrepreneur the list of investors who received the company's executive summary. After this, the network steps back from the process in deference to the independent nature of its investors, and in consideration of the securities laws it would invoke by going any further.

Entrepreneurs may keep their companies on the network for six months to a year and may periodically update the listing. The longer a company is listed, the more leads and inquiries it's likely to generate. Consider listing your company if the network can provide the names of possible investors to call or if it can prequalify you for at least 25 matches.

◆ **Ace-Net.** This is the "mother of all networks." Ace-Net is a private capital network, national in scope, that is designed to match entrepreneurs seeking capital with *accredited* individual investors. It was developed by several private venture capital networks and the Small Business Administration (SBA) with assistance from the Securities and Exchange Commission (SEC), as well as state securities regulators.

Ace-Net is not for the faint of heart. To "list" on the network, a company may have to complete a SCOR (Small Company Offering Registration) form, also known as a U-7, which, when complete, looks suspiciously like the detailed prospectus that companies file before going forward with an initial public offering (IPO). In addition, once a SCOR is filed, state securities regulators can raise some thorny issues—such as whether potential specific investors satisfy minimum net worth figures set by the states. *(See Appendix C for a brief overview of securities regulations.)*

Ace-Net relies upon existing private capital networks to act as "nodes" or feeders. Started in late 1996, Ace-Net boasts nine nodes that entrepreneurs can contact to get a registered offering on the system. Though still in its formative stages, Ace-Net is one of the most promising capital-formation tools ever to emerge in the United States.

ACE-NET FEEDER NODES

Betty Kadis, Executive Director
Technology Capital Network at MIT
P.O. Box 425936

Cambridge, MA 02142
617-253-2337
FAX: 617-258-7395

David H. Gerhardt, Executive Director
The Capital Network
3925 West Braker Lane, Suite 406
Austin, TX 78759-5321
512-305-0826
FAX: 512-305-0836

Wayne Hodges, Director
Advanced Technology Development Center
Georgia Institute of Technology
430 Tenth Street, Suite N-116
Atlanta, GA 30318
404-894-3575
FAX: 404-894-4545

William Otterson, Director
UCSD-CONNECT, MS-0176F
Extended Studies & Public Service
University of California, San Diego
La Jolla, CA 92093-0176
619-534-6114
FAX: 619-552-0649

Terrence H. Hicks
VP, Entrepreneurial Services
Ben Franklin Technology Center
3625 Market Street, Suite 200
Philadelphia, PA 19104
215-382-0380
FAX: 215-387-6050

David Day, Marketing Director
KTEC-Kansas Technology Enterprise Corporation
214 SW Sixth Street, Suite 100
Topeka, KS 66603-3719

913-296-5272
FAX: 913-296-1160

Keith Blurton, President
MERRA
2901 Hubbard Road, Suite B106
Ann Arbor, MI 48105
734-930-0033
FAX: 734-930-0145

Alex Glass, President
Bay Area Regional Technology Alliance
39550 Liberty Street, Suite 201
Freemont, CA 94538
510-354-3902
FAX: 510-354-3903

Stash Losowski, Director
NJIT Enterprise Development Center
105 Lock Street
Newark, NJ 07103
973-643-5740
FAX: 973-643-4502

You can also visit Ace-Net's Internet site, at **https://ace-net.sr.unh.edu**, which contains hyperlinks to several of the feeder nodes.

◆ **Academics.** Another avenue to angels is through business schools with entrepreneurship programs. Bard Salmon, one of the architects of Ace-Net and a board member of the Technology Capital Network at MIT, says that universities with good entrepreneurship programs teem with venture activity. More important, professors have contacts with angels who are anxious to get a crack at promising companies. *(See Appendix B for a list of top university-based entrepreneurship programs.)*

"The relationships between professors, the businesses they are helping to create, and investors is not widely promoted or obvious, but it is very definitely there," says

Salmon. "Outreach and telephone calls to these professors, who are often sympathetic to any kind of entrepreneurial activity, is an effective way to get connected to the school's venture forums, educational programs, and networking events, which in turn leads to contact with angels."

According to Bob Tosterud, executive director of the Council of Entrepreneurship Chairs, a nonprofit group located at the University of South Dakota, even schools with relatively new entrepreneurship programs attract top professors with significant contacts in business and finance. "My advice would be to get the catalog of any nearby university to see if they have entrepreneurship programs," says Tosterud. "If so, call the professor and schedule a meeting."

(Buy the September 1997 issue of Success *magazine for its annual survey of the "Best Business Schools for Entrepreneurs." To order back issues, call 800-967-2083. Editorial offices can be reached at 212-883-7100.)*

◆ **Professional services firms.** There are two things just about every venture capital deal requires: legal advice and accounting services. Because of this, law and accounting firms know the private investors in their market. Moreover, professional services firms sell access to these investors either implicitly or explicitly as part of their fees. If your attorney or accountant cannot provide access or introductions to individual investors, consider finding new professionals.

This sounds like harsh advice, especially if your attorney or accountant has been a loyal and competent adviser over the long haul. However, if bringing in outside investors is totally outside the sphere of their practice, your decision to raise money means you may have outgrown these relationships. Thus, the entire relationship may require reevaluation, and sadly perhaps, a parting of the ways.

Planning Your Approach to Angels

THE JOB OF CONVERTING LEADS INTO INVESTORS IS THE MOST difficult, challenging, and time consuming part of the process. However, just throwing time at the task won't carry the day.

To prevail, you must *plan* and work smart. Two of the smartest people in the business are Miles Spencer and Paul Rosenbaum. Spencer is creator of *Money Hunt*, a show about raising money that airs on public television stations around the country. Rosenbaum, managing director of Wayland Partners, of Wayland, Massachusetts, has created and run three high-octane companies and was one of the general partners of American Research and Development (ARD), the oldest venture capital partnership in the United States. ARD pioneered the concept of early-stage-technology investing by backing Digital Equipment Corp. and earning billions for its investors.

Spencer and Rosenbaum recommend a broad-based strategy to convert angels to your side:

◆ **Form an advisory board.** You need to clearly define the business and industry you are in. Armed with this information, reach out to those who have succeeded on a grand scale in the business and ask them to serve on an advisory board. Rosenbaum says there are psychological reasons why people readily agree to such a proposition. Among them are an appreciation for being recognized as a success, a desire to relive success vicariously, and an altruistic urge to provide the kind of support they wish they had had during the early days of their own venture.

The ideal advisory board consists of three to five individuals who are well connected in an entrepreneur's industry. Many times, companies have advisory boards with 10 or 12 members; these tend to be unwieldy, and as a result, ineffective. By contrast, boards with three to five members can and should convene quarterly. Generally, advisory boards are not compensated with cash, but are incentivized with options.

Kenneth Taylor, a board member of Johnson Controls, and a principal in Milwaukee-based Sullivan Associates, which conducts board-of-director searches, says that the best way to assemble an advisory board is to start with a written mission or vision statement and to recruit people for specific tasks. "The main thing," he says, "is don't waste your time building an advisory board for prestige. Build it to help you accomplish something."

An advisory board will help generate leads and increase the confidence that would-be investors have in your team. When you sign up advisory board members, Rosenbaum says, "you'll find it's a very natural process for them to open up their Rolodexes. You might even find one of them will take the lead on getting you in front of people they know."

◆ **Obtain a lead investor.** If you are raising $1 million, you might just run into the one investor who will write a check for the entire amount; however, the odds are against it. In most cases, you will find an investor who wants half or one-quarter of the deal. It's wise to find this person first, because he or she will serve as a magnet to draw in other investors.

For example, Katherine Hammer and Robin Curle, cofounders of Evolutionary Technologies International, Inc., a data management firm in Austin, Texas, landed one of the major figures in their community as a lead investor who, in turn, attracted others. Hammer and Curle set up shop in the Austin Technology Incubator. According to Hammer, the founder of the incubator was George Kozmatsky, who was also the founder of Teledyne, the technology giant. "George provided us with unbelievably helpful counsel and guidance," recalls Hammer. He also provided introductions to an informal network of angels who were affiliated with the incubator. One of these investors was retired Admiral Bobby Inman, who committed $250,000—20 percent of what they were looking for—that in turned helped the pair secure an additional $1 million from other investors.

◆ **Secure legal counsel.** The act of raising money may invoke several federal and state securities laws. Even though many private transactions are exempt from federal and state securities laws, there can still be a myriad of requirements regarding notification, offering memoranda, and the number of investors that can participate in the offering. The task of raising capital is difficult enough. Don't add to your burden by unknowingly running afoul of securities laws.

◆ **Have a deal summary and a business plan.** Spencer suggests sending a summary of the company to investors before they receive your telephone call. This summary must, in just one page, describe the company, the product or service, the market, competition, key personnel, funding required, use of proceeds, and key historical and projected financial information. Consider writing a paragraph about each of the above categories.

You must have a complete business plan for two very good reasons. First, if the initial contact is successful, the investor will request one. Says Spencer, "You definitely don't want to try writing a business plan after the request is made. When an investor asks for your plan, it needs to be on his or her desk the next morning."

Second, it's only by writing a business plan that you can possibly hope to answer the kinds of questions that an investor will ask. *(Flip ahead to Chapter 9, which discusses how to write a business plan. At the beginning of the chapter are 50 questions a well-written plan should answer. If you cannot answer these questions, you are not ready to call investors.)*

◆ **Figure out your sizzle.** "The business plan is your steak," says Rosenbaum, "but you will need some sizzle in your oral pitch to make an emotional mark on the investor." For instance, computer products manufacturer Xyplex, Inc., of Boxborough, Massachusetts, raised a lot of money privately before it went public and was acquired. Rosenbaum says that rather than trying to drag investors through a tortuous technical explanation of the company's product, the executives of the company said, "We are the company that turbocharges your DEC Vax computer."

Another Rosenbaum client, Active Control Experts of Cambridge, Massachusetts, developed and manufactured so-called smart materials. But rather than confusing investors with the underlying concepts of piezoelectronics, the company piqued investors' interests with the positioning statement: "We are the company that puts the brains in the skis."

Even Wall Street uses this trick. When venerable motorcycle maker Harley-Davidson went public, the pitch to investors was: "Own a piece of an American icon."

◆ **Line up references.** You will also need to collect allies with whom investors can speak. These might be customers, potential customers who have said they will buy your product or service when it's available, the executive director of your trade association, members of your advisory board, or other investors. One of the keys to successfully corralling investors is to commit them to ever larger and more important actions. Convincing them to call someone else about your deal can be the first step in that process.

◆ **Get warm-body introductions.** If you get the names of investors you don't know, Spencer says it's vital to get what he calls a "warm-body" introduction. "Avoid contacting someone out of the blue at all possible costs," he counsels. Former employees, trade associations, accountants, lawyers, or the person who supplied you the lead in the first place, all represent viable candidates to help with your initial contact.

Initiating Contact

AS THE PRECEDING STEPS SHOW, A LOT OF PLANNING MUST GO into raising money. According to angel investor Ron Conway, a member of a San Francisco group called the Band of Angels, "Entrepreneurs fail to raise money in most instances not because their idea isn't viable, but because they haven't adequately planned the details, of which there are many." However, once the proper planning has been done, it's time to dial for dollars and initiate contact. Here's what you will need to do:

◆ **Qualify the investor.** The investor will ask you very early on in your initial conversation who you are and what your company does. In response, your positioning statement should include a concise description of what you're looking for and why. You should say, for example, "Well, our firm makes computer products that turbocharge Vax computers, and we're raising $1 million to roll out the products we just beta tested." At this point, says *Money Hunt*'s Spencer, you also need to determine if the investor deals in companies such as

Does Your Angel Qualify?

IF YOU HEAR any of these responses, the angel may not be for you:

◆ I don't invest in technology companies.

◆ I don't invest in low-technology companies.

◆ I only invest in companies with revenues.

◆ I only invest in companies with positive net income.

◆ I only invest in foreign companies doing business in the United States.

◆ My investments are restricted to an industry that you are not in.

◆ My investments require your personal guarantee.

◆ I only invest in companies in which I have influence over product development.

◆ I only invest in situations where the company has a strategic alliance with my company.

◆ I only invest in private offerings of public companies.

yours. "Unlike investment bankers and institutional venture capitalists, whose criteria and preferences are published in numerous references, angels are largely unknown," he says. If the person you are talking to doesn't invest in your type of business, Spencer says, "you need to give that investor a kiss goodbye. But before you do, ask for the names of three investors who would like your deal."

◆ **Prepare to answer questions.** If investors want to talk, they'll ask a lot of questions. Some of these questions will be about details, such as: "Why do you use a Post Office box instead of a street address?" Others will be more global in nature: "Does the Internet represent a threat to you, or does it represent a viable new distribution channel?"

Whatever the question, your answer should be persuasive and exude confidence. Remember, the angel is evaluating you from the moment the conversation begins. Unlike lenders who rely on cash flow to get their money back, angels rely on the ability of the entrepreneur to sell the company again and again to other equity investors and ultimately to investment bankers for a public offering, or to a corporation that will buy the company outright. The upshot is, if you can't be convincing to this investor, he or she will conclude that you probably can't convince the next investor down the road and that ultimately, his or her investment will remain trapped inside the company.

Another reason that all of your answers must sound confident during the initial phone conversation is that investors want assurance that their capital will go to work right away, and not lie fallow while you figure out fundamental aspects of your business. According to Rosenbaum, this is where all of the pain and suffering of putting together a good business plan, as well as the planning of the sales effort, pay off. "If you started calling investors without being prepared like this, you would be wasting your time," he says.

◆ **Get a commitment to meet.** Ultimately, your objective during the initial contact is to get a meeting with the investor. Rosenbaum says that if you are working with a well-qualified list of investors—people who are or were involved in your industry—you should get a meeting 50 percent of the time. If your initial target list was less focused, then he says you might expect to generate a meeting with just 25 percent of those whom you initially contact.

By the way, if you work in a hovel, it may not be a good idea to let an angel see the dirt floor. If this is the case, tell the angel, "There's not much to see here." Instead, suggest neutral territory, such as a restaurant, hotel, or your accountant's or attorney's office.

If investors are interested in your business, they will need more information in the form of a business plan. However, according to Rosenbaum, simply agreeing to send out the plan cedes control of the process to investors. It is far better, he says, to make a face-to-face meeting a condition of sending out the business plan. "You want the investor to agree to meet at a specific future date after he has received and reviewed the business plan," says Rosenbaum.

Spencer says that the business plan should arrive on the investor's desk the next morning by overnight mail. In addition, the package might include some kind of sample or tangible evidence of your product or service. If you are distributing toys, this is simple enough. It's a bit more difficult if you build mobile homes. Even in difficult situations, it's worth considering creative solutions, because, as Spencer says: "Papers pile up on peoples' desks and get lost, whereas objects and samples get played with, looked at, and talked about."

Most experts, Rosenbaum and Spencer included, counsel that if the investor is reasonably qualified to participate in the deal, you should never take no for an answer during the initial contact over the telephone. Spencer says that many investors will purposely be difficult to get ahold of or evasive in their phone conversations just to determine an entrepreneur's commitment and aggressiveness. "They want to get an idea of how hard you would work with their money if they funded the business," he says.

Rosenbaum, on the other hand, suggests that 60 percent to 70 percent of the time investors decline an opportunity, it's because they don't understand a certain aspect of the product, the market, the technology, or your vision for the company. "When somebody says no," he states, "you've got to ask them why, and then educate them, teach them, and try to show them where their thinking is off."

Winning at the Initial Meeting

ENTREPRENEURS SHOULD HAVE TWO OBJECTIVES FOR THEIR initial meeting with angels.

First, to get angels to like them. Second, to get them to commit to taking some kind of action step.

For the deal to happen, the investor must like the entrepreneur—not truly, madly, deeply, but fundamentally—because personal chemistry is the cornerstone of the relationship between angel and entrepreneur. For many angels, the motivation to invest is psychological, as well as economic. Accordingly, entrepreneurs would do well to review the concepts outlined in part two of *How to Win Friends and Influence People*, by the late Dale Carnegie. Naturally, making these concepts part of your fiber takes a lifetime of practice. However, simply committing yourself to them the morning of a meeting with a private investor could spell the difference between success and failure. As spelled out originally in 1936, these ideas are:

1 Become genuinely interested in other people.
2 Smile (!).
3 Remember that a person's name is to that person the sweetest and most important sound in any language.
4 Be a good listener. Encourage others to talk about themselves.
5 Talk in terms of the other person's interests.
6 Make the other person feel important—and do it sincerely.

BEING GENUINELY FRIENDLY WILL HELP; HOWEVER, MAKE sure you've prepared a formal presentation. In every area of the capital markets, the 20-minute pitch is standard operating procedure. Accordingly, walk into your meeting prepared to deliver no more than a 20-minute, but thorough, presentation. *(See Chapter 9 for helpful details on the effective presentation of business plans.)*

Most meetings with angels are one-on-one, or perhaps a-

Action Steps for Close of the Initial Meeting

GET THE INVESTOR to:

◆ Call your references
◆ Conduct due diligence about your industry, technology, products, or service.
◆ Try your product or service.
◆ Have his or her accountant look at your historical or projected financials.
◆ Read your business plan.
◆ Interview some of your key personnel, vendors, or advisers over the telephone.
◆ Look at competitive product or service offerings.

few-on-one, if the angel asks some friends to join in. As a result, the best way to present to angels is to walk them through a set of 10 to 12 slides that present the highlights of the company, the market, and the deal. During your presentation, investors may interrupt to ask questions. This is fine. The presence of the slides will continuously allow you to get back on track.

Unless you are totally bereft of human intuition, you will know whether or not to try to seal the investor's commitment during that first meeting. In general, though, first meetings, like most first dates, do not result in a commitment. Consequently, your objective for the first meeting is simply to get the investor to commit to some kind of action step.

Getting the investor committed to an action step sets the stage for the second—and potentially closing—meeting. The close for the first meeting, however, should go something like: "Okay, you're going to try our product and talk to some of our customers. That will probably take two weeks. Let's agree to meet on this date, and discuss what you've found out and your reactions to it."

Money Hunt's Spencer says that nothing motivates investors so much as the thought that they might get left out of a deal that other investors are in. "You've got to walk a very fine line here," says Spencer. "You've got to let the investor know you're on a fast track, but that you will not shut them out of the deal if they are genuinely interested in investing."

Closing the Deal at the Second Meeting

THE SECOND MEETING IS THE OPPORTUNITY TO GET THE investor involved in the decision-making process. According to Selling 101, the date for the second meeting should have been set during the first meeting. If it wasn't, getting the second meeting might take quite a few phone calls. Remember, the angel might be playing hard-to-get simply to see how aggressive you might be if you were working with his or her money.

Regardless of how you get there, however, the second meeting is deal time. It's best to have some good news to start things off, such as mentioning other investors who are interested in the deal or reporting progress on any operational front. However, after that, it's time to look for a commitment.

According to Rosenbaum, one approach that often proves successful in "popping the question" is to get the investor involved in the decision-making process. "If you can do that," says Rosenbaum, "you're almost home." Here's how a hypothetical closing might go, according to Rosenbaum's recommended approach:

ENTREPRENEUR: "We've met twice now, and you've had a chance to think about our situation a little bit more and read our business plan. You have a firm grasp of what we are trying to accomplish. For all these reasons, I'd like to ask your advice on something. How much capital do you think we should be raising?"

INVESTOR: "Well, your plan says that you're looking for $1 million. But I think that ramping up for demand and accounts receivable is going to eat a lot more cash than you anticipate. I think you would do better with $1.5 million."

ENTREPRENEUR: "That's one of the reasons I'm trying to bring experienced investors like yourself to the table, because I think in the long run good advice is as important as capital. (Resist the urge to breathe in.) Okay, of that amount, how much can you commit to?"

If the angel is interested, he or she will probably talk numbers. If he or she won't commit, well, that's a small victory, too, since it will save you from wasting any more time. However, if the angel is interested and responds with a promise of $250,000 to $500,000, you have accomplished your objective of securing a lead investor.

If the angel commits to the entire funding, then the deal is highly negotiable. If it's less—and it probably will be because most angels dislike being in a deal alone—then you will have to specify some sort of deal structure on what's called a "term sheet." Spencer says that a term sheet focuses the angel on specific issues—the timing of the investment, the amount of equity the investor receives, the level and frequency of financial reporting, and so on—that must be understood for the deal to close. A term sheet also has almost incalculable value when it comes to getting other investors into the deal because there is often a herd mentality among angels. "With one term sheet," says Spencer, "you can get five more."

How One Company Did It

MANAGEMENT AT LAHEY HITCHCOCK CLINIC, OF BURLINGTON, Massachusetts, one of the largest physician group practices in the country, saw a massive opportunity in providing total automation solutions for home care agencies. The nonprofit group even spun out a for-profit affiliate, CrystalView, Inc., of Waltham, Massachusetts, to fully capitalize on the situation, says Bruce Nappi, who left his post as director of advanced technology at the clinic to become president of CrystalView.

Nappi's first task was to raise the required funding for the new enterprise. Though he had never raised capital before, Nappi enjoyed a critical advantage that would give him the stamina the task required: He remained on the clinic's payroll while working on the job of fund-raising. This gave Nappi the freedom to treat fund-raising as a full-time job.

After a brief and unrequited stint looking for institutional venture capital, and then a corporate investor, Nappi targeted individual investors and structured a $2 million offering that was exempt from federal securities laws. It enabled him to sell securities to an unlimited number of accredited (read "wealthy") and nonaccredited (read "pretty wealthy") investors.

Starting in the first quarter of 1997, Nappi spent two months laying the required groundwork. He wrote a business plan, formed an advisory board, created a positioning statement ("We provide turnkey solutions for home care automation . . ."), and lined up would-be customers to talk to would-be investors. He even sought legal counsel. Testa Hurwitz, a Boston legal powerhouse, stepped up to the plate with deferred fees and a list of contacts.

Thus armed, Nappi went about generating leads with textbook grace. His first source was nearly 20 years of business cards he had collected from vendors, colleagues, and others.

"I selected 400 people for letters and got a great response," he says. In fact, Nappi got the deal's first lead angel when an old acquaintance called him after receiving the letter and said, "I'll get my family together and put some money in." This investor put up $160,000 and gave Nappi 40 more names, which generated three more investors. Meanwhile, his original 400 letters turned up five more angels.

Another one of Nappi's original contacts led him to a professor in the entrepreneurship program at Boston University's Medical School. This investor wrote a sizable check and then gave Nappi 40 more names to work with. These 40 names brought in five more investors. By then, Nappi had some $250,000 from 15 investors sitting in an escrow account.

The third vein came from one of the clinic's physicians, who recommended that Nappi meet a neighbor of his who frequently got involved with early-stage companies. This person promptly joined CrystalView's board of directors. "He didn't invest per se," says Nappi, "but he helped refine our business plan, and with the refinements in place, gave us a good list of investors to send the plan to under his name." Nappi says this pulled in five more investors. At this point, Nappi had 20 investors in the deal.

The fourth big break came through a venture capital forum sponsored by the Technology Capital Network at MIT, though it happened in an unexpected way. Nappi made a 15-minute pitch before 100 or so investors. He said the response from the audience was enthusiastic, but that the presentation itself did not generate any investors. "The funny thing was, after the meeting the four of us who had presented, all being pretty much in the same boat, swapped leads," he says. "That list I took away from the meeting brought in the rest of the investors I needed to close on the deal's $625,000 minimum."

Nappi says that during the process, he kept his goals focused and limited. "The objective of my first phone call was simply not to let my initial letter go unanswered," he says. "If the investors were talkative, I tried to qualify them. If they qualified, I simply tried to get them to look at the business plan." Nappi estimates that just 5 percent of all contacts agreed to look at his business plan. The good news was that 50 percent of investors who looked at the plan agreed to a meeting.

Though the numbers were daunting, Nappi says that he wasn't too aggressive with anyone on the phone. "The experts tell you not to take no for an answer," he says, "but my feeling was, all these leads came from personal relationships, and I wasn't going to burn any bridges by being overbearing or a hard sell on the telephone."

During the first meeting, Nappi's objectives were again limited and focused. "I went in simply trying to build stature with the investors and to give them a sense of confidence in what we were doing," he says. Nappi generally closed meetings by making a commitment that he would get back to the investors. "None of them seemed ready for me to contact them at a specific date or time," he says. "They had some undefined process they had to go through to think things over."

The task of getting back in touch with potential investors was a big one, requiring between two and 10 calls each. Once the calls were made, Nappi stopped his pursuit when an angel began to raise serial and unconnected objections. Nappi says, "When they said, 'If you can get me a letter from one of your clients that says they will do business with you when you're funded,' and then when that was done, they said, 'I need some kind of primary market research,' I knew I was wasting my time and would be better off cutting this investor loose.

"The funny thing was," he says, "that people who were genuinely interested moved pretty quickly. The ones I leaned on, or spent a lot of time with, rarely turned out so well."

Types of Angels

TO BE SUCCESSFUL IN A SEARCH FOR CAPITAL, YOU MUST understand the mind-set of your would-be angel. Personal chemistry and economics will carry the day. However, personal chemistry might have an edge. Many angels will alter their investment criteria and standards if they develop a strong, trusting bond with an entrepreneur.

To help close the deal, says Rich Bendis, president of the Kansas Technology Enterprise Corporation (KTEC), entrepreneurs need to understand investors' personality types. Bendis speaks from experience; a former venture capitalist, he took a company public and with the proceeds from the eventual sale of the company ascended to the realm of the angels himself. Bendis says that while private investors come in many different shades, they can be broken down into five basic types:

◆ **Corporate angels.** Typically, so-called corporate angels are senior managers at Fortune 1000 corporations, who have been laid off with generous severances or have taken early retirement. For instance, in Bendis's neck of the woods, Marion Labs and Sprint created an entirely new generation of wealthy corporate executives in Kansas City. Corporate angels may say they are looking for investment opportunities, but in reality they are looking for another job. This doesn't mean they won't invest. Bendis says these investors typically have about $1 million in cash and may put $200,000 into a deal.

In addition to the cash, an entrepreneur may get the corporate angel himself to occupy some senior management position, such as in business development. While corporate angels will work for free, after about six months they tend to get nervous watching their remaining nest egg, which took them a lifetime to build, stop growing, or worse yet, shrink. Psychologically, corporate angels can make for a poor fit because after a lengthy and successful corporate career, the reality of a truly entrepreneurial organization can be a shock to the system. This drawback notwithstanding, corporate angels can help an organization evolve from seat-of-the-pants entrepreneurial management to professional management.

Corporate angels typically make just one investment (unless their last one didn't work out, and there's still enough cash and gumption left to have another go). With respect to the one investment they do make, corporate angels tend to invest everything at once. That is, they invest all the cash they are ever going to invest up front, and get nervous when the hat gets passed their way again.

◆ **Entrepreneurial angels.** These are the most prevalent investors. Most of them own and operate highly successful businesses. Since these investors have another source of income, and perhaps significant wealth from an initial public offering (IPO) or partial buyout, they will take bigger risks and invest more capital. Whereas corporate angels are looking for a job, entrepreneurial angels are looking for synergy with their current business, a way to diversify their portfolio, or, in rarer instances, a way to prepare for life after their current business no longer requires their attention. The best way, therefore, to market your deal to these angels is as a synergistic opportunity.

As a result of this orientation, entrepreneurial angels seldom look at companies outside of their own area of expertise and will participate in no more than a handful of investments at any one time. Because of their rather narrow focus on certain industries in which they have experience, this type of angel can contribute in terms of industry contacts, sales leads, technical expertise, and contacts among sources of capital.

Entrepreneurial angels almost always take a seat on the board of directors but rarely assume management duties. They will make fair-sized investments—typically $200,000 to $500,000—and invest more as the company progresses. However, because of their own agendas, when the synergy or the potential they initially perceived disappears, often so do they.

◆ **Enthusiast angels.** While entrepreneurial angels tend to be somewhat calculating, enthusiasts simply like to be involved in deals. Bendis says that most enthusiast angels are 65 or older, independently wealthy from success in a business they started, and have abbreviated work schedules. For them, investing is a hobby, and, as a result, they typically play no role in management and rarely seek to be placed on a board. Since these angels are hobbyists, they tend not to invest so much in technologies or industries as they do in people and ideas. Since they spread themselves across so many companies, the size of their investments tends to be small—from as little as $10,000 to perhaps a few hundred thousand dollars. On the plus side, however, enthusiasts tend to have a difficult time saying no and often will bring their friends into a deal. While they do not need the rich return often required by entrepreneurial investors, the enthusiast is in continual search of the one company that will go public.

◆ **Micromanagement angels.** Micromanagers are very serious investors. Some of them were born wealthy, but the vast majority attained wealth through their own efforts. Unfortunately, this heritage makes them dangerous. Since most have successfully built a company, micromanagers attempt to impose the tactics that worked for them on their portfolio companies. Though they do not seek an active management role, micromanagers usually demand a board seat. If the business is not going well, they will try to bring in new managers.

It's possible to exploit the behavior patterns of micromanagers, but at a cost. Specifically, they enjoy having as much control as possible and will pay for it by putting more capital into the business. Because they micromanage the companies they fund, these investors limit their efforts to perhaps four companies at any one time. Like entrepreneurial angels, micromanagers can be valued-added investors; however, the expertise they bring to the table can quickly become a burden as well.

These traits suggest a strategy for dealing with micromanagement angels: Establish "rules of engagement" up front to see if they are willing to live by them and structure the deal so that one party can buy out the other if fatal incompatibilities arise.

◆ **Professional angels.** The term "professional" in this context refers to the investor's occupation, such as doctor, lawyer, and, in some very rare instances, accountant. Professional angels like to invest in companies that offer a product or service with which they have some experience; a doctor will look at medical-instrumentation companies, a franchise attorney will look at franchise deals, and so on. They can offer additional value when they offer legal, accounting, or financial expertise for which a new company would otherwise have to pay hefty fees.

These investors tend not to need to know what's going on in the business day to day, and they do not micromanage their portfolio companies. In fact, professionals rarely seek a board seat. However, they can be unpleasant to deal with when the going gets rough and may believe that a company is in trouble before it actually is. They are good for initial investments, but are less likely to make follow-up investments.

Professional angels will invest in several companies at one time, and their capital contributions range from $25,000 to $200,000. They tend to have more comfort investing with their peers. Thus, a professional investor will likely offer a pathway to others. You can accommodate them by offering to make a presentation before several of their friends so that they can provide input to the investor afterwards.

It is important to keep in mind that most angel investors fly below the radar screen of conventional corporate finance. Consequently, as a business person, you read and hear a good deal more about deals involving venture capitalists, merchant bankers, and investment bankers. However, don't be fooled into thinking these are the most appropriate or abundant sources of capital. For the vast majority of small businesses—perhaps as much as 90 percent of them—angel investors represent the most viable and appropriate way to go.

Kinds of Angels

1.) Corporate Angels

2.) Entrepreneurial Angels

** 3.) Enthusiast Angels
        - invest in people

4.) Micromanagement Angels

* 5.) Professional (Lawyers, doctors etc.) Angels
        - like to invest in areas they are
        familiar with.

CHAPTER 3

Initial Public Offerings

HE SEARCH FOR PRIVATE EQUITY CAPITAL
among angel investors is a numbers game. The
more angels an entrepreneur contacts, the greater
the chance of success. However, other numbers
suggest that this type of capital, though plentiful, is
not abundant enough.

In the same way that insurance companies and
pension funds allocate just a tiny fraction of their
assets under management to venture capital
partnerships, so, too, do angels allocate just a small
portion of their wealth to venture investments. An
angel investor who puts $250,000 in a deal but is
trying to keep illiquid, high-risk investments to just 5
percent of his or her portfolio, has about $5 million
in assets. For entrepreneurs seeking capital, these
numbers present a significant challenge. How many
multimillionaires can they hope to meet? If their
close rate is 10 percent, they would need to contact a

large number of wealthy individuals.

This challenge is one of the main reasons that public offerings are a viable option for smaller companies. Though public investors tend to invest much smaller amounts than angels, there are many, many more public investors. In addition, their investment standards are not nearly as rarefied as those held by angels.

This chapter explores conventional initial public offerings, or IPOs, which are deals underwritten by an investment banker and which trade on a recognized stock market. This technique, though popularized by the business press, is difficult and unrealistic for many companies. As a result, readers are urged to carefully read the section in this chapter about the pitfalls of IPOs, as well as the following chapter, which shows alternative approaches to tapping public investors for growth capital.

Top 10 Reasons to Go Public

GOING PUBLIC USUALLY SEEMS LIKE A PRETTY GOOD IDEA. There are several aspects to recommend it. The following are the oft-cited 10 commandments for IPOs:

1 Proceeds from a public offering are permanent. Unlike a loan, the funds do not have to be paid back.

2 A large amount of capital can be raised at one time. Rather than receiving, say, $1 million from a private offering, companies can get $5 million to $15 million or more in one shot.

3 Once public, companies gain direct access to the capital markets and can raise more capital by issuing additional stock in a secondary offering.

4 Public companies can use their common stock as currency to acquire other companies. Companies frequently cite "growth through acquisition" as the primary expansion strategy in their IPO prospectuses.

5 Public companies can more easily attract and retain skilled employees by using their common stock—typically in the form of options—as a carrot.

6 Public ownership delivers a certain level of prestige that private companies do not have.

7 Going public provides owners and founders liquidity for their holdings in the business. For entrepreneurs approaching retirement, an IPO makes estate planning dramatically easier and a lot more enjoyable.

8 Public companies enjoy a higher valuation than private enterprises. Consider that as the third quarter of 1997 came to a close, the companies comprising the S&P 500 were, on average, valued at 16.5 times their earnings, while most business brokers will tell you that private businesses may sell for one to five times their cash flow. That's less than half the public valuation, largely because there is little liquidity for investors in a private company.

9 Public companies are more attractive acquisition candidates. For some companies, the strategy is to grow to the point where they become an attractive middle-market acquisition candidate and then to sell out.

10 Going public usually makes you a millionaire. Even if you initially don't get the price you want, playing the waiting game can be profitable. The late An Wang, founder of Wang Labs, was once asked if he was upset that investment bankers priced his company at $15 per share in the initial offering. His reply, according to popular lore: "Whatever for? I didn't sell any of my stock until it hit $80."

As the chart below shows, an increasing number of business owners apparently believe that they will benefit from an IPO.

Forget for a moment that even in a great year, like 1996, only 872 companies made it through the IPO gauntlet. Later on, this chapter explains the difficulties associated with the process of going public and some of the structural flaws associated with being a small, public company. For the moment, let's assume you want to raise more than $7.5 million and take your company public in the conventional fashion. Your first and most important task is to find an investment banker who can do the job.

SOURCE: SECURITIES DATA COMPANY, NEWARK, NJ

Number and Dollar Volume of Initial Public Offerings by Year

YEAR	AMOUNT RAISED ($ BILLIONS)	NUMBER OF OFFERINGS
1991	16.8	368
1992	24.1	517
1993	41.3	708
1994	28.5	612
1995	30.2	583
1996	49.9	872
1997	43.3	624

The Universe of IPO Underwriters

THE WORLD OF INVESTMENT BANKING IS REGULATED BY professional conventions that border on a caste system. To see it at work, look closely at a "tombstone" advertisement. Notice how the members of the syndicate—that is, the listing of securities firms participating in the offering—appear in alphabetical order from left to right, and how there are several groups of alphabetical listings in the tombstone advertisement. Each group is known as a "bracket." By and large, the song and dance of deal syndication is played out on these brackets. However, brackets also offer a handy nomenclature for helping entrepreneurs understand who's who and what's what among investment bankers in terms of candidates for an IPO. Below is a listing of brackets and the kinds of deals they typically do:

◆ **The majors.** These are sometimes called "bulge-bracket" firms, referring to their dominance in underwriting syndicates. Household names such as Merrill Lynch; Salomon; Smith Barney; Prudential Securities; and Goldman, Sachs & Co. have elaborate investment banking operations, and court Fortune 1,000 and international businesses. This is not to say that these firms avoid IPOs for emerging businesses. However, the ones they look for are relatively young companies that hope to dominate a developing market, such as wireless service in eastern Europe, or Internet services via cable. If a business needs $50 million and may someday need $1 billion, it's a perfect candidate for a bulge-bracket underwriter. The majors generally underwrite IPOs ranging from $25 million to $250 million, and these offerings represent a small segment of their overall business.

◆ **Specialty firms.** There are a select few specialty firms that often share space with the bulge bracket firms in underwriting syndicates. These firms include NationsBanc Montgomery Securities, Hambrecht & Quist, BancAmerica Robertson Stephens, and BT Alex. Brown, to name a few.

These underwriters raise capital for leading-edge technology companies at early stages of development. They also frequently have some sort of specialty in a nontechnology business, as well. For instance, Montgomery is strong in banking and finance, while BT Alex. Brown tends to be a mecca for emerging trucking and transportation companies.

While firms such as BT Alex. Brown appear to rival the majors because of significant IPO activity, in reality many were, until recently, much smaller. Consider that while Alex. Brown boasted capital of more than $350 million prior to its acquisition by Bankers Trust, according to the Securities Industry Association handbook, Merrill Lynch has capital of more than $20 billion. The so-called specialty firms were, in fact, regional brokerages. However, the explosion of technology-driven IPOs, and the acquisition of many of these firms by banks, has changed their role and the dynamics of investment banking.

Specialty firms tend to serve institutional investors and are hard pressed to underwrite companies that will have market capitalizations of less than $100 million after the offering is complete. Specialty firms usually underwrite IPOs from $15 million to $75 million. In most cases, the companies these firms take public have been through several rounds of institutional venture capital. Initial offerings represent a major portion of their business.

◆ **Regionals.** Every major metropolitan area has one or two "regional" investment banking firms. These firms, by definition, take great interest in local companies. Though they are further down on the investment-banking food chain, most regionals are surprisingly large, owing to the fact that many were weaned on the rich municipal- and corporate-bond businesses that sprouted in their backyards. They also have vast retail networks—some with more than 1,000 brokers—and, in many instances, a muscular institutional business, as well. Unfortunately, the size and scale of regional firms sometimes makes them a poor fit for smaller, emerging companies. Regionals handle IPOs ranging in size from $12 million to $50 million. They are most interested in companies in their own area—which can be defined as a state or an area the size of the eastern seaboard—that seem capable of becoming solid, middle-market businesses with annual revenues ranging from $50 million to $500 million. Generally speaking, IPOs represent a small part of a regional's work. The more active firms do three to five IPOs a year, while others may take a company public once every other year.

◆ **Boutiques.** Boutique brokerages, as they are sometimes called, defy generalization. Some are quite powerful. For

Top 25 IPO Underwriters of 1996

UNDERWRITER	AMOUNT RAISED ($ MILLIONS)	NUMBER OF IPOS
GOLDMAN, SACHS & CO.	$9,888	51
MORGAN STANLEY DEAN WITTER	7,237	47
MERRILL LYNCH & CO.	3,624	38
SMITH BARNEY, INC.	2,991	34
DONALDSON, LUFKIN & JENRETTE	2,497	29
ALEX. BROWN & SONS	2,472	51
LEHMAN BROTHERS	2,415	29
CREDIT SUISSE FIRST BOSTON	1,906	14
SALOMON BROTHERS	1,644	19
MONTGOMERY SECURITIES	1,303	34
ROBERTSON STEPHENS	1,204	28
J.P. MORGAN & COMPANY	1,003	13
HAMBRECHT & QUIST	964	30
BEAR, STEARNS & CO.	846	14
COWEN & CO.	608	17
WILLIAM BLAIR	560	11
NATWEST MARKETS	522	11
DILLON, READ	510	14
PAINEWEBBER	438	10
OPPENHEIMER & COMPANY	399	14
PRUDENTIAL SECURITIES	377	7
FRIEDMAN, BILLINGS, RAMSEY & CO.	327	13
FURMAN SELZ	317	7
UBS SECURITIES	314	9
NESBITT BURNS SECURITIES	262	1
TOP 25 TOTALS	44,629	545
MARKET TOTALS	50,013	874

instance, New York City–based Allen & Company, headed by media and entertainment adviser Herbert Allen, is considered by many to be a boutique. Some refer to Wasserstein, Perella & Co. as a merger and acquisition boutique. By and large, however, boutique firms are small, relatively unknown

Top 25 IPO Underwriters of 1997

UNDERWRITER	PROCEEDS ($ MILLIONS)	NUMBER OF ISSUES
GOLDMAN, SACHS & CO.	$6,784	39
MORGAN STANLEY DEAN WITTER	5,329	42
MERRILL LYNCH & CO.	5,072	36
CREDIT SUISSE FIRST BOSTON	2,431	19
J.P. MORGAN & COMPANY	2,332	9
DONALDSON, LUFKIN & JENRETTE	2,162	25
SALOMON SMITH BARNEY	2,031	31
FRIEDMAN, BILLINGS, RAMSEY & CO.	1,900	11
LEHMAN BROTHERS	1,675	22
NATIONSBANC MONTGOMERY SECURITIES	1,317	32
BEAR, STEARNS & CO.	1,295	10
BT ALEX. BROWN	1,206	24
PRUDENTIAL SECURITIES	979	12
BANCAMERICA ROBERTSON STEPHENS	712	18
HAMBRECHT & QUIST	518	16
J.C. BRADFORD	468	4
SBC WARBURG DILLON READ	445	3
PAINEWEBBER	430	6
RAYMOND JAMES & ASSOCIATES	354	9
COWEN & CO.	307	9
ING BARINGS	263	4
ABN AMRO HOARE GOVETT	259	1
CIBC WOOD GUNDY SECURITIES	255	8
A.G. EDWARDS & SONS	253	10
UBS SECURITIES	235	8
TOP 25 TOTALS	**39,012**	**408**
INDUSTRY TOTALS	**43,330**	**624**

SOURCE: SECURITIES DATA COMPANY

outside of the trade, and concentrate either on a particular industry or a particular kind of transaction. Many boutiques concentrate on IPOs. While the skill and expertise of the regional powerhouses is uniformly high, there is a wide variance among the boutiques. Some are quietly making untold millions for investors on a select group of carefully screened deals, while others are pumping out IPOs and keeping the securities regulators hopping. Boutique IPOs range from $5 million to $20 million, but usually fall between $8 million and $10 million. At many boutiques, IPOs are the central focus, while a secondary emphasis involves market making for Nasdaq-traded stocks.

In 1996 the average size of the 545 IPOs underwritten by the 25 largest firms was $81 million ($44.6 billion/545 offerings). During the first half of 1997, the average of the 163 IPOs done by the dominant firms was $93 million ($15.2 billion/163). Both of these averages, though high, are illustrative. Most of the household names in investment banking don't look at IPOs between $5 million and $15 million because the offerings aren't large enough to generate the required fees and aftermarket trading profits.

What the rankings do not reveal is who's doing all the other deals. It's important to find out, since, in 1996, these other deals represented 40 percent of the IPO market. The average size of these deals was $16 million, a reasonable amount for many smaller companies looking for capital. The lion's share of these offerings was underwritten by boutique brokerage firms, many of which specialize in IPOs for embryonic companies, as well as small but established ones.

The lesson: If your company is a rising star, and you envision that after an IPO it can be valued at more than $100 million (the number of shares multiplied by the stock price), aim for the majors, the specialty firms, or—to be a big fish in a little pond—the regional underwriters. If your company is a shooting star, and you envision that after an IPO it will be valued at less than $100 million, target the boutiques and regionals in your search for an investment banker.

Finding IPO Underwriters

A NUMBER OF DIRECTORIES PUBLISH LISTS OF INVESTMENT bankers. However, such volumes offer little help for entrepreneurs because many investment bankers do not provide services for small companies. Unfortunately, some entrepreneurs looking for capital don't know any better. They pursue these bankers anyway and end up running into dead ends.

If you cold call investment banking firms, the likelihood they will guide your company through an IPO is almost nil. Sure, it happens, but the odds are against it. According to Cliff McFarland, a principal with the Houston-based investment banking firm McFarland, Grossman & Company, "There are very few underwriters I know that will seriously consider even *looking* at a business plan that they do not have at least some connection with."

While cold calling is generally unproductive, mass distribution of a business plan to potential investment bankers can be downright damaging. The ploy works well with angels, who, as a practical matter, don't talk with one another and derive comfort from having others in the deal. However, in the investment banking world, deal makers communicate with each other all the time. When a company is shopped around to many firms at once, investment bankers tend to find out and recoil. Worse yet, when discussing such a company with their peers, investment bankers frequently miscommunicate important concepts and actually undermine an entrepreneur's chances of success of getting an audience with an underwriter.

The appropriate channel to investment bankers who can take your company public are professional advisers including attorneys, accountants, and in rare instances, financing consultants.

The Big Six accounting firms—Price Waterhouse, Arthur Andersen, Ernst & Young, Coopers & Lybrand, KPMG, and Touche Ross—are the dominant players when it comes to IPOs. Since accounting issues are often the most complex and time-consuming elements in an IPO, these firms have close and long-standing relationships with investment bankers. As a result, referrals from Big Six accountants almost always result in face-to-face meetings with investment bankers. According to Bob Fish, a partner with Coopers & Lybrand in New York City, "Connections with and referrals to investment banking firms is part of what we are selling. It's the value-added component that we can bring to the table."

Chances are, your accountant will recommend a firm that you didn't consider. However, use the benchmarks in the following section titled "Evaluating IPO Underwriters" to get an idea of how good your accountant's referral really is. Incidentally, this is where the choice of a Big Six accounting firm pays off. Since they are national in stature, these firms can make referrals in all 50 states.

Here's how it works, according Coopers & Lybrand's Fish: "If you are in New York and want to meet with underwriters in San Francisco, you have the partner in charge of your account call the West Coast and find out who worked on the last five IPOs there," he says. "Your partner simply

Top 10 Accounting Firms Ranked by IPO Proceeds

1997 RANK	COMPANY	PROCEEDS ($ MILLIONS)	NUMBER OF DEALS
1	ERNST & YOUNG	8,318	121
2	KPMG PEAT MARWICK	8,313	82
3	ARTHUR ANDERSEN & CO.	7,383	118
4	DELOITTE & TOUCHE	5,517	61
5	PRICE WATERHOUSE	5,244	67
6	COOPERS & LYBRAND	4,097	61
7	GRANT THORNTON	494	14
8	PISTRELLI, DIAZ Y ASOCIADOS	350	1
9	P.N. SOONG & CO.	260	1
10	MORET ERNST & YOUNG & CO.	259	1

requests that the San Francisco staff make the required introductions."

If your chosen Big Six firm is active in a region, the conversation on your behalf should go something like this: "Hello, Bill? Listen, I wanted to alert you to something. We're having one of our clients back East send you their business plan. We just thought it was a situation you might be interested in. . . Yes, we do the audit work for them. . . No, I talked to our partner there. He says the guy who runs it is a very solid guy. So, listen, keep a heads-up for this business plan. I'll follow up with a call."

Fish, who works in Coopers & Lybrand's high-tech/venture capital practice in New York, says he makes similar calls on behalf of clients all the time. He's quick to warn that opening a door doesn't mean a deal will get done. It simply means the banker will take the call. Sometimes, however, that's the hardest part.

If your accountant can't help, another path to an investment banker is through attorneys. Every IPO has at least two sets of lawyers: one for the company and one for the under-

1996 RANK	NUMBER OF DEALS	1995 RANK	NUMBER OF DEALS
3	168	3	107
4	118	4	68
2	154	1	91
6	81	2	44
5	90	6	69
1	107	5	74
7	18	10	8
20	1	N/A	10
N/A	N/A	N/A	N/A
N/A	N/A	13	N/A

SOURCE: SECURITIES DATA COMPANY

writer. When there's more than one underwriter on a deal, as there frequently is, then there are even more lawyers. Like accountants, certain attorneys frequently have close relationships with investment bankers. In most cases, the underwriters genuinely trust the attorneys and pay close attention to deals that they refer.

The following charts, compiled by the Washington Service Bureau, of Washington, D.C., shows the law firms doing the most deals for issuers and underwriters during

Top 15 Issuer's Counsel of 1997

FIRM	VALUE OF REGISTRATION ($ MILLIONS)	NUMBER OF IPOS IN REGISTRATION
SULLIVAN & CROMWELL NEW YORK, NY 212-558-4000	8,906	11
SHEARMAN & STERLING NEW YORK, NY 212-848-4000	7,668	9
CLEARY, GOTTLIEB, STEIN & HAMILTON NEW YORK, NY 212-225-2000	6,027	9
O'MELVENY & MYERS LOS ANGELES, CA 213-669-6000	1,828	10
LATHAM & WATKINS LOS ANGELES, CA 213-891-1200	1,509	10
SKADDEN, ARPS, SLATE, MEAGHER & FLOM NEW YORK, NY 212-735-3000	1,381	13
PAUL, WEISS, RIFKIND, WHARTON & GARRISON NEW YORK, NY 212-373-3000	1,340	5

the first half of 1997. Ranking is by the number of deals in registration.

In the same way that lists of leading IPO underwriters can be misleading, so, too, can lists of professional advisers. Since a number of highly active law firms don't make the charts, entrepreneurs need to dig a little deeper. To find attorneys with IPO experience, visit the SEC's Edgar Web site at **www.sec.gov/edgarhp.htm** or a professional or trade library that subscribes to the *SEC*

FIRM	VALUE OF REGISTRATION ($ MILLIONS)	NNUMBER OF IPOS IN REGISTRATION
GOODWIN, PROCTER & HOAR WASHINGTON, DC 202-974-1000	1,314	6
WILSON, SONSINI, GOODRICH & ROSATI PALO ALTO, CA 415-493-9300	1,227	23
VINSON & ELKINS HOUSTON, TX 713-758-2222	1,058	8
WACHTELL, LIPTON, ROSEN & KATZ NEW YORK, NY 212-403-1000	965	4
MORGAN LEWIS & BOCKIUS PHILADELPHIA, PA 215-963-5000	963	8
SIMPSON, THACHER & BARLETT NEW YORK, NY 212-455-2000	929	4
DAVIS POLK & WARDWELL NEW YORK, NY 212-450-4000	919	6
LEBOEUF, LAMB, GREENE & MCRAE NEW YORK, NY 212-424-8000	916	3

SOURCE: SEC NEW REGISTRATIONS REPORT

New Registrations Report, published by the Washington
Service Bureau, 655 15th Street, NW, Washington, DC;
800-955-5219.

Top 15 Underwriter's Counsel of 1997

FIRM	VALUE OF REGISTRATION ($ MILLIONS)	NUMBER OF IPOS IN REGISTRATION
SHEARMAN & STERLING NEW YORK, NY 212-848-4000	9,233	20
SKADDEN, ARPS, SLATE, MEAGHER & FLOM NEW YORK, NY 212-735-3000	7,536	24
CLEARY, GOTTLIEB, STEIN & HAMILTON NEW YORK, NY 212-225-2000	5,790	6
DAVIS POLK & WARDWELL NEW YORK, NY 212-450-4000	4,842	17
SULLIVAN & CROMWELL NEW YORK, NY 212-558-4000	4,002	13
SIMPSON, THACHER & BARLETT NEW YORK, NY 212-455-2000	2,725	17
FRIED, FRANK, HARRIS, SHRIVER & JACOBSON NEW YORK, NY 212-859-8000	1,610	7

Using Financing Consultants

ANOTHER ROUTE TO AN INVESTMENT BANKER IS THROUGH
financing consultants. Using consultants is controversial
and at times risky. Some consultants are unqualified. Others
overshop a company and actually undermine its chances of
success. Still others are prohibitively expensive.

FIRM	VALUE OF REGISTRATION ($ MILLIONS)	NUMBER OF IPOS IN REGISTRATION
BROBECK, PHLEGER & HARRISON SAN FRANCISCO, CA 415-442-0900	1,533	26
BROWN & WOOD NEW YORK, NY 212-839-5300	1,425	7
GIBSON, DUNN & CRUTCHER LOS ANGELES, CA 213-229-7000	1,181	9
CRAVATH SWAINE & MOORE NEW YORK, NY 212-474-1000	1,125	9
HOGAN & HARTSON WASHINGTON, D.C. 202-637-5600	1,076	4
LATHAM & WATKINS LOS ANGELES, CA 213-485-1234	1,063	9
DEWEY BALLANTINE NEW YORK, NY 212-259-8000	921	7
WILSON, SONSINI, GOODRICH & ROSATI PALO ALTO, CA 415-493-9300	883	21

SOURCE: SEC NEW REGISTRATIONS REPORT

For example, Ytzik Grossman, a financing consultant with Target Capital of New York City, takes an equity position of 2 percent to 9 percent in client companies. In addition, if he is successful in taking a company to the public markets, Grossman gets an annual retainer of $100,000. "There's no doubt about it," says Grossman, "I'm expensive. But I get results. The underwriters I work with trust me, and my deals go to the head of the line."

Is hiring a consultant a good idea? For entrepreneurs who are sophisticated, know what they are doing, and have the time to see the effort through, the answer is probably no. However, for entrepreneurs who have less experience raising money and do not have a lot of time, the answer is a qualified yes.

The advantage a consultant offers is comparable to the value an insurance agent brings to the table. With intimate knowledge of several carriers, an agent can often do a better job of finding insurance than customers can on their own. But just as a bad insurance agent will get you bad insurance, a bad financing consultant will likely get you undesirable financing. So, here's what to look for and do:

◆ **Structure fees carefully.** Contingency arrangements—deals in which consultants are paid a percentage of the funds they raise—may save on monthly fees, but several things can go wrong. First, if prolonged effort is required, consultants who do not see any cash flow may run out of steam. Second, the consultant might push a certain transaction, not because it's in the best interest of the client, but because it's the fastest route to the closing table and the fee. Third, entrepreneurs tend to ignore the advice of professionals whom they are not paying. This can cause the consultant to become prematurely discouraged and often leads to the collapse of the relationship.

The ideal fee structure is often a modest monthly retainer, perhaps $1,500 to $2,500 per month. Combine this with a success fee, usually a percentage of the capital raised, or with smaller deals, an equity stake in the company on the back end.

In the case of a public offering, investment bankers sometimes refuse to pay intermediaries because it reduces the amount of compensation they are able to earn from a deal as a result of National Association of Securities Dealers (NASD) regulations. Many investors want all of the proceeds working for the company instead of paying off financial intermediaries.

Experienced consultants know this, of course, and shop their deals to sources of capital that protect their fees. However, the final deal may go to investors the consultant has never worked with. Situations can get sticky, with the entrepreneur actually mediating between the would-be investors and their own consultants.

You can avoid many of the problems associated with equity-based compensation by having consultants buy their equity cheaply before the search for capital begins. The problem is that if the consultants don't produce, the entrepreneur has unwanted, and sometimes cantankerous, minority shareholders. The whole process is structurally imperfect, and as a result, plain, old fees are sometimes the best way to go.

Make sure you have a 60-day out-clause in the contract. If you aren't in front of sources of capital within this time frame, something is wrong, and your deal is probably floundering.

Check references. It's amazing how many entrepreneurs hire consultants without looking into their past. Speak to the principals of three firms for whom the consultant has worked. Did the consultant add value? Did she do what she said she would? Most important, did she raise the money?

The complete absence of codified professional standards when it comes to raising money probably accounts for the voluminous number of financing consultants. Anybody can hang out a shingle and do it. This doesn't mean that all financing consultants are unqualified, but it does mean that some of them are.

Evaluating Investment Bankers

THE QUALITY OF INVESTMENT BANKING SERVICES VARIES significantly from bracket to bracket and from firm to firm. The endpoints run from superior to scandalous. Even professional advisers who recommend investment banking firms are not always aware of how good the firm really is. Since the costs of filing, to say nothing of consummating, an IPO are in the neighborhood of $200,000, entrepreneurs must be able to critically evaluate underwriters. Can the underwriter get the company to the closing table? Can the firm do it with a minimum amount of trauma?

Below is a methodology to help evaluate the skill of investment banking firms and the likelihood that they will be interested in your deal. Collect the following information on each IPO handled by your target underwriters over the past year or two. Much of the data you need are available at **www.ipocentral.com**. This information exists in a much more manageable form in *Going Public: The IPO Reporter,* published by IDD Enterprises, L.P., New York City.

Data needed to evaluate IPO underwriters:

1 Initial offering price range
2 IPO price
3 Percent difference between range and actual price
4 Number of days in registration
5 Earnings per share of the company at the time the underwriter took it public, and associated price-earnings ratio
6 Price of the shares or units two to three months after the offering

Underwriters that have done just one IPO over two years are probably not good candidates to handle your mission. There are many possible reasons for their low IPO count. They may have gone out of business, or their one offering may have been a disaster either in the market or perhaps internally. Perhaps they don't even do IPOs as a general rule but underwrote one offering because of unique circumstances.

Underwriters that have completed two IPOs over the past two years, however, are good candidates. New issues are hard to do, and a one-deal-per-year-clip is a respectable pace. Such an underwriter is in a position to devote a substantial portion of its resources to supporting deals in the aftermarket. However, firms that do just one IPO per year are pretty choosy about the company they eventually commit themselves to.

Boutique underwriters that have completed four to eight offerings over the past two years are even better candidates. While these firms clearly know the craft, bringing one offering to market each quarter has several implications, so caution is required. First, the corporate finance personnel or principals at these firms are on overload all of the time, and, as a result, are very difficult to reach and to sell to. Second, new offerings they accept may get short shrift while they're busy working on other deals. Third, with so many offerings in the aftermarket, they may not have the capital to provide meaningful support.

For these underwriters, check to see how many offerings they put in registration but never completed, the number of days their issues spent in registration (more than 135 days on a consistent basis spells trouble), and how many of their issues are trading above their offering price. Generally speaking, you should disregard geography. Unlike private investors whose interest is generally confined to a radius of no more than a three-hour drive, boutiques usually have national connections.

Regardless of which type of underwriter you investigate, the following analysis will help you identify the best candidates for your deal, as well as the the attendant risks:

◆ **Look at earnings per share of the underwriter's IPO candidates.** If all of an underwriter's offerings have been for companies with positive earnings, and your company has no earnings—or worse, has losses—there's probably not a match.

◆ **Look at the aftermarket performance for each of the underwriter's deals.** If they are all way up, say more than 50 percent, it's an indication that the firm prices its offerings too cheaply. Remember, if you sell 60 percent of the company for $10 million, and the price more than doubles in the aftermarket, it means the same amount of capital might have been raised by selling only 30 percent of the company. An underwriter's miscalculation will cost a company's founders precious points of equity. On the other hand, if their deals are way up, it could indicate irregularities in the underwriter's trading practices. Finally, if the underwriter's deals show a pattern of dipping below their IPO price three months after the offer, it indicates an inability to support their issues in the aftermarket. The ideal aftermarket performance would be a 10 percent to 15 percent premium in the share price during the first three months after the offering commences trading.

◆ **Look at the difference between the filing range and the eventual price of the IPO.** The filing range is just that, the range of prices at which the issue may come to market according to the preliminary prospectus, and is generally expressed as something like: "$9 to $11," or "$5.50 to $7.50." Does the underwriter show a pattern of filing at $6 to $8 per share, or unit, and then bringing its deals to market at $5? Sure, market conditions may have played a role in the price reductions. But such a pattern may also mean the underwriter plays hardball by threatening to pull the plug on the deal at the last minute unless the company accepts a lower price.

◆ **Try to spot industry preferences.** It is unlikely that among boutique brokerage firms you'll find any. However, if a brokerage firm seems to favor a particular business or type of company that matches your own, it's more likely they'll want to talk to you.

◆ **Look at how many offerings the underwriter took into registration but never completed.** The costs of filings are too high to risk on an underwriter that leaves them at the alter. In addition, investment bankers resist completing someone else's broken deal, so if you file but don't make it, your company is damaged goods.

Courting the Underwriter

THE INITIAL COURTSHIP BETWEEN COMPANIES AND UNDERwriters works best when it's governed by certain conventions. Following these rules helps to avoid immediate and inappropriate rejection. And make no mistake, it is a courtship that takes time, money, and patience. Take note:

◆ **Inspire confidence that you can pull it off.** Given all the hurdles it takes to go public, it's a miracle that any firms ever do. Investment bankers know this. Therefore, they're looking not only for solid companies but for entrepreneurs who can move mountains. According to investment banker John Lane, "A mediocre company with can-do management will more often go public than a great company with naive management."

◆ **Don't try to negotiate the investment banker's fees.** Compensation is regulated by the NASD, and for deals under $15 million the bankers take the maximum allowable compensation. Period.

◆ **Disclose problems you have up front.** Even though you might be putting up $250,000 to $500,000 to get the deal done, by the latter stages of the offering the underwriter is in just as deep. Therefore, as a matter of practice, most investment bankers commission a detailed background check before they issue a letter of intent. If this check turns up irregularities that you tried to conceal, kiss your offering goodbye. Besides, showing your warts voluntarily makes you more human, and in some instances, actually helps forge a bond.

◆ **Show you can sell.** Your underwriter will depend on other underwriters to get the deal done. If the investment banker senses you can't get other underwriters excited about your offering, his or her interest will significantly wane.

Selling skills are also important for aftermarket trading. In many ways, that's when the selling *really* begins. When the investors who bought into the IPO are ready to realize profits, there has to be a pool of new investors that want to buy the shares. If there isn't, then the underwriter knows it will have to dip into its own capital to buy the shares coming onto the market. Therefore, you've got to inspire confidence that you can keep selling the company once it starts trading.

◆ **Don't attempt to hide the fact that you want to get rich.** This is a turnoff because the underwriter knows that's exactly why you want to go public. By trying to hide this fact you demonstrate a less than candid attitude. Even if your goals are not purely monetary, keep them in check; if you don't, the underwriter will question whether you are driven by the proper set of motivations. After all, which race-car driver would you like to back: the one who wanted to win or the one that simply liked driving fast?

◆ **Don't argue about the value the underwriter places on your company without good information.** Your choices here are pretty limited. Swallow hard, or walk. *(To learn about valuation strategies, see Chapter 7.)*

◆ **Show you are in it for the long haul.** Underwriters can't sell a deal in which the management isn't going to be around in 18 months, so they don't bother trying. If, during the initial conversation with the investment banker, you say, "My idea was to flip this deal to the public and then move on to something else," then moving on is exactly what you will end up doing. Only sooner rather than later.

◆ **Don't tell tall tales.** If your sales are zero today but will be $350 million next year, the underwriter will probably end the phone call fast, given all the work you have to do.

◆ **Don't attempt to negotiate the sale of your own shares in the IPO.** It happens all the time, in larger, more developed companies. However, for smaller IPOs, it's rare; the underwriter and prospective investors feel better about the risk associated with the investment if you are keeping all of your own chips on the table. It never hurts to ask, but if you make the sale of your own shares a condition of the negotiations, then negotiations may come to an abrupt end.

◆ **Never burn a bridge.** No means no. However, it also means maybe. The fact is, most IPOs take so long to shop that when all is said and done, investment bankers who said no when you first started may say yes a year later. Many times, their objections to an absence of earnings, incomplete management team, or unproven product will be overcome in the intervening time, so there's good reason to call the banker back and rekindle discussions.

Regrettably, how to move from the initial contact with an investment banker to a letter of intent and then to a deal is beyond the scope of this work. Companies that are in serious discussions with underwriters should have a team of advisers that includes the board of directors, as well as counsel and auditors with IPO experience, to help guide them through the process.

In fact, if these advisers are truly doing their job, they should have already filled in company founders on all the reasons an IPO may be a bad idea. For some companies, the IPO is, as Winston Churchill so elegantly put it, not the beginning, nor the end of the beginning, *but the beginning of the end.*

Maybe You Shouldn't Go Public

PERHAPS THE BEST REASON NOT TO GO PUBLIC IS THAT SO very few companies successfully negotiate the process. One explanation is that the investment bankers who typically underwrite early-stage companies raising between $5 million and $15 million have almost the same growth hurdles as venture capitalists—that is, compound annual increases in earnings of at least 25 percent.

Another reason that so few deals close is that most investment bankers who underwrite IPOs are unwilling to take risks on perfect strangers. There is plenty of legal exposure even when they've identified all the warts. Therefore, in the majority of cases, investment bankers end up working on deals that are in some way already wired into their own network of personal contacts. Incidentally, this goes a long way toward explaining how, if investment bankers are so choosy about the companies they finance, so many incredibly unworthy companies get underwritten.

But one of the primary reasons you shouldn't try to go public is because most deals die before they even get filed. Oftentimes, market conditions wipe out a slew of deals that are in the pipeline and ready to go. However, many more offerings topple in the negotiation stages or during the process of drafting a registration statement. In short, tens of thousands of deals never even see the light of day. According to Sandy Robertson, founder and chairman of BancAmerica Robertson Stephens, which has raised some $50 billion for emerging growth companies since its founding in 1972, "There is a wide, but essentially predictable range of reasons that initial public offerings do not get past the registration or drafting stage." Robertson's top reasons include:

- **Disagreements on valuation.** The company and the underwriter cannot agree on the valuation of the company. The owners think they have the next Microsoft. The bankers have heard this a million times. "Even though initially you are negotiating a range of valuations," says Robertson, "this is the toughest issue that the bankers and the entrepreneurs have to agree on, and oftentimes they don't."

- **Vanishing profits.** The company is sporting a set of financial statements that, when restated in response to more conservative accounting policies, go from reporting profits to reporting losses.

- **The love affair is over.** "Sometimes a certain sector will go too far, too fast," says Robertson. "When the valuations get too frothy, there can be a sell-off, which hurts all of the similar companies in registration." For instance, the rash of recent Internet-related deals, and their poor aftermarket performance, left investment bankers with a sour taste in their mouths for similar upstarts.

- **The deal drags on too long.** Robertson says that IPOs that hang around too long get shopworn. "When a deal doesn't come when it's scheduled," he says, "it sends a signal that the underwriter may be having trouble with it."

- **Deteriorating financial performance.** If the negotiations drag on too long, and the company's fortunes decline, it can kill the deal. Regrettably, faltering financial performance is often directly attributable to the amount of time management has spent shopping and negotiating the offering.

- **Regulators get tough.** Robertson says that sometimes companies get caught in the cross fire between government and regulators, causing the deal to implode. For instance, the Department of Defense has, in the name of national security, limited the disclosures of a certain contractor filing a registration statement. Unfortunately, the SEC, which is sworn to uphold the Securities Act of 1933, cannot declare the offering effective without these disclosures. Ultimately, it may cause the demise of the deal.

In addition, sometimes a nuance of a particular offering will prevent it from getting clearance in a state that is critical to the underwriters. The most well-known example of this is the case of Apple Computer, which could not sell its IPO in Massachusetts.

◆ **Personalities clash.** "If the investment banker and the chief executive can't get along," says Robertson, "it's highly unlikely the company will file a registration statement with the investment banker's name on it."

IN ADDITION TO THE REASONS CITED BY ROBERTSON, WHICH are endemic to all IPOs, there are other obstacles that kill deals of $15 million or less before they start. These include:

◆ **Failed salesmanship.** The owners and senior management of the company prove they are unable to sell the deal to other underwriters that will be part of the selling group or syndicate. The lead underwriter can't do the deal alone.

◆ **Expenses are too high.** The company cannot afford the $250,000 "dry-hole" expenses for legal, audit, and printing fees. Many times, underwriters offer bridge financing to help the issuer over the hump with expenses. Bridge deals are often structured as a loan with warrants. However necessary, bridge financing is expensive for issuers. And if the deal doesn't fly, the company still has to find a way to pay back the loan.

◆ **Lockup agreement.** The investment banker insists that founders and other inside shareholders "lock up" their shares—that is, not sell them on the open market for a period of two years—and the founders refuse to go along. This strategy is designed to limit the amount of shares coming into the market that the underwriter might have to buy, and to a lesser extent, to increase the credibility of the offering.

Even if a company sidesteps all the above obstacles and completes an offering, it can still founder in the aftermarket. In the most straightforward terms, it comes down to this: *There are several structural reasons why tiny companies that go public will see their share prices decline over time rather than rise.* When this happens, all of the reasons to go public in the first place—such as easy access to capital, estate planning, a currency for acquisitions—become null and void. Here are some of the structural problems:

◆ **Intense competition.** This is one of the primary challenges that place continuous downward pressure on so-called microcapitalization stocks. There are 3,300 stocks trading on the New York Stock Exchange (NYSE); 750 on the American Exchange; 6,500 on Nasdaq (plus another 5,800 issues trading on Nasdaq's Bulletin Board); and some 6,300 mutual funds. Each of these securities is competing for the attention and the investment dollars of investors.

The upshot is that all but the most hyped new stocks—and, of course, household names—are virtually invisible to most of the individual investors who can buy them. Even when, per chance, investors hear about the stock, the investor's thinking might run something like this: "Let's see, I can buy Microsoft, which trades over five million shares a day and whose biggest problem seems to be the threat of antitrust action from having cornered the market. On the other hand, I can take a flyer on this company I barely know, trading in the lower depths of the market with potentially revolutionary, but as yet unproven, technology." In this mind-set, even if a company is doing well, it can languish, its price inching downward, as investors, edgy over the lack of action, continue to put in sell orders.

As a case in point consider U.S. Transportation Systems, Inc. (Nasdaq: USTS), which manages the transportation needs of corporations. With solid earnings growth over the past three years and the transition in earnings from a net loss in 1993 and 1994 to an average net income of over $1 million per year in 1995 and 1996, USTS still can't get any respect from the market. With a price/earnings ratio hovering just over three times trailing earnings at this writing, USTS stock seems cheap. In fact, considering that the average price/earnings ratio for a Dow transportation stock was 15.4 at the dawn of 1997, USTS is getting just 20 percent of the valuation that the market offers similar companies.

Will the market ever fully value USTS? The landmark work on valuing stocks, *Security Analysis: Principles and Technique,* by Benjamin Graham and David Dodd, postulates that the market will always find value in a stock no matter how obscure the issue may be. This notion still holds true today and is the cornerstone idea for hundreds of billions of dollars under management. But old Graham and Dodd were canny; they never said *when* or *how long* it would take the market to recognize the true value of a stock. For many tiny companies that are public with their stock way underwater, it seems to take forever.

◆ **Limited capital.** Beyond intense competition, a deal can also founder if the investment banker's capital is limited. Most entrepreneurs believe that once their company is public, market forces will take over and naturally regulate the price of their stock. However, once chief executives come face-to-face with the invisibility of their deal, they begin to see just how important, and in most cases, just how inadequate, their investment banker's capital is.

Here's what happens: Three months after the initial offering, all of the shares so carefully placed with other brokerage firms and with the leading underwriter's best customers, start to come back on the market through sell orders. Because the deal is tiny, gets little attention, and has no major Wall Street research coverage, there are no buyers—except, of course, the leading underwriter, which has a major stake in the offering and a damaged reputation if the deal flounders. But how much stock can the underwriter take in? The amount depends on several factors, but mostly on the underwriter's willingness to tie up its own capital, putting stock in inventory.

There are two key words in the above sentence. The first is "willingness." Spencer Marcum, an investment banker in Denver, once remarked, "The problem with most brokerage firms is that they think they are in the moving business, when in reality, they are in the storage business." Many underwriters, he says, are simply not willing to take in and hold stock for a prolonged period of time.

The second key word is "amount." Consider for a moment the numbers involved. The underwriter sells one million shares at $8 per share, and the issue trades up to $10. Now 200,000 shares come back onto the market through sell orders. Does the underwriter have $2 million in capital it is willing to tie up buying these shares? The answer is that most underwriters doing $8 million offerings don't have enough capital to support all of their deals.

In fact, of the 478 brokerage firms that are members of the Securities Industry Association—clearly not all brokerage firms, but definitely a good sample and one that supposedly represents the *larger* firms—two-thirds have less than $15 million in capital. Many of these firms have less than $1 million in capital.

The underwriter's likely response, therefore, to the 200,000 shares coming back on the market is to lower the bid at which it is willing to buy "loose" stock and minimize the hit to its capital. This lowering of the bid is, in fact, a decline in the price of the stock, which often sends a ripple of fear through investors, causing still more shares to come onto the market. The new sell orders put further pressure on the bid, and the downward spiral begins.

◆ **Large capitalization orientation.** Yet another reason a completed deal can fizzle is the market's focus on large-capitalization stocks. One way to measure the change in scale of the U.S. stock markets is to look at the inflated definition of *small-capitalization*, or *small-cap*, companies. In the late 1980s, small-cap stocks were those with market capitalizations of less than $100 million. In the early 1990s, the term came to mean those with market capitalizations of $100 million to $250 million. While there are still some investors that stick with the neoclassical definitions, today it's not uncommon to find money managers running small-cap funds that are buying stocks with valuations of $500 million to $1 billion.

One of the primary reasons for this inflation has been the institutionalization of the capital markets. What does this mean? Individuals are investing more through mutual and pension funds—that is, institutions—than they are on their own. According to the Investment Company Institute in Washington, D.C., 36.8 million U.S. households own mutual funds, a 20 percent increase over mid-1994.

While individuals derive substantial benefits by investing this way, it has dramatically changed the character of the market. Specifically, when mutual-fund managers have, say, $500 million under management, they might take positions of $2 million to $10 million in portfolio companies. When these companies have market capitalizations of $300 million, the portfolio manager can easily trade in and out of positions without affecting the price.

But what about when the company has a market capitalization of $15 million? For the same portfolio managers with $500 million to manage, really small companies are no longer feasible investments. It's like a Formula One racer on a go-cart track; there simply isn't enough room for them to move in and out of the traffic—at least, not without causing the kind of accident that might hurt themselves and a lot of other drivers on the track.

The damage wrought by this institutionalization, from a capital-formation perspective, is twofold. First, it has taken a lot of individual investors out of the market. Second, it means that all of the liquidity (i.e., the ease with which shares can be bought and sold) in very small stocks is limited to the remaining few individual investors who don't have the wherewithal to create an active trading market for all of the public companies out there.

Company performance, market conditions, and supply and demand may mean little when it comes to the price performance of a microcapitalization stock. What may ultimately determine the price is the amount of capital the underwriter has and is willing to put on the line.

Can you live with all these potential pitfalls? The benefits are certainly there: prestige, quick access to capital, a currency for making acquisitions, a carrot for attracting skilled employees, and the possibility of becoming a millionaire are all achievable with a public offering. The huge risk is that if the stock doesn't do well—and there are a whole lot of reasons unrelated to the actual performance of the company why it might not—these benefits may become more difficult to realize than if the company simply stayed private.

For some entrepreneurs, the structural inadequacies of the market are not a problem. If they can grow the company with that one, vital trove of cash, then á la Graham and Dodd, perhaps the stock will one day reach a full and fair valuation.

As a case in point, investment banker Tony Petrelli of

Denver, Colorado–based Neidiger/Tucker/Bruner Inc., recalls his client, Simula, Inc., manufacturer of crash-worthy aircraft components such as aircraft seating systems. Simula went public in April 1992 by raising $5 million, with Neidiger as one of the lead underwriters. "We priced the company very conservatively," recalls Petrelli. Conservative, indeed. At the time of the offering, Simula had a market valuation of just $11.9 million. Today it trades on the NYSE and has a market valuation of more than $150 million. "Simula provides a textbook example of how small companies can succeed by going public," says Petrelli.

Since its initial offering, Simula raised additional equity in private offerings and utilized its growing equity base to raise additional debt financing. In addition, as the stock responded to the improving financial performance, Simula was able to use its common stock as a currency to consummate two acquisitions.

Founders and shareholders have been well rewarded in the process as well. Based on prices in early 1997 and adjusting for stock splits, Simula's common stock is trading at $25.50 per share, five times its IPO price. Founding shareholder Stanley Desjardins has seen his equity stake in the company grow to more than $61 million.

Stories like Simula's feed the dreams of starry-eyed entrepreneurs who see a public offering as a launching pad for their company. The rewards are well known; however, as the preceding analysis suggests, entrepreneurs should understand the considerable business risks involved in the process, as well.

CHAPTER 4

Alternatives to an IPO

THE DEGREE OF DIFFICULTY ASSOCIATED WITH initial public offerings (IPOs) is unfortunate.

It keeps many companies from accessing public investors. It also prevents public investors from cashing in on promising companies by financing them very early in their development the way professional venture capitalists do. On a happier note, however, this barrier generally insulates public investors from the kinds of risks and losses institutional venture capitalists face.

The real tragedy for entrepreneurs, however, is that there are other, often overlooked, ways to access public investors. In many respects, these techniques are more appropriate than conventional offerings. Chief among these alternative techniques are reverse mergers, exempt public offerings, and direct public offerings.

Reverse mergers and certain exempt offerings

rely upon the idea that public companies, even ones without much of a trading market, can raise capital more easily than private companies that have no market whatsoever for their shares. Create a public vehicle, and the opportunities for raising capital become dramatically easier.

The third technique, direct public offerings (DPOs), is, as the name implies, a way for companies to raise capital themselves without the aid of an investment banking firm. DPOs are no easier than IPOs. However, company founders and senior management—rather than a third party, such as a brokerage firm—control the process. For many entrepreneurs, the comfort of being in charge is preferable to having to rely upon the competency of others.

Reverse Mergers

THE IDEA BEHIND A REVERSE MERGER IS SIMPLE: A PROMISING private business becomes public by acquiring or merging with an already public—though usually dormant—company.

A textbook example of a successful reverse merger involves LCA-Vision, Inc., of Cincinnati, Ohio. LCA founder Dr. Stephen Joffe already had a profitable hospital-based management business. However, he saw an exciting opportunity in establishing freestanding centers offering laser refractive eye surgery, a procedure that corrects nearsightedness. There was just one hitch: The process was awaiting approval by the Food and Drug Administration (FDA). "The U.S. market," according to Joffe, "might be as much as $10 billion and should grow as patient acceptance of the process increases." While waiting for federal approval, LCA-Vision laid plans for financing the huge rollout of surgical centers in the United States and acquired an interest in a laser surgery center in Toronto where the same process already had been approved.

Contemplating his options for financing alternatives, Joffe felt a straight IPO was possible, but highly unlikely for a new and untested concept. Joffe believed he could convince an underwriter of the potential. However, would an underwriter be able to convince other investors of Joffe's potential? What would happen if FDA approval was delayed? With only one center in operation, wasn't Joffe's company really a start-up?

On the other hand, with a reverse merger Joffe only had to convince the controlling shareholder of a public shell that the reward was worth the risk. That he was able to do. In the ensuing transaction, Joffe acquired shares in the shell company in exchange for his contribution of the operating assets of LCA-Vision. At the end of the process, Joffe had a majority position in the shell company, and the shell company had the operating assets of LCA-Vision. The public company then promptly changed its name to LCA-Vision to reflect the new direction of the business.

The deal was completed in August 1995. Sure enough, the FDA approved LCA's laser refractive procedure two months later, and Joffe was off in a sprint. Almost immediately after completing the reverse merger, Joffe raised $485,000 privately. Then he used his publicly traded common stock to purchase the remaining interest in the surgery center in Toronto. These funds, combined with favorable lease terms on surgical laser equipment, helped Joffe open surgery centers in Cincinnati, New York City, Cleveland, Savannah, Baltimore, Dayton, and Toledo. After a brief honeymoon on Nasdaq's Bulletin Board, LCA-Vision moved up to the Small-Cap market in January 1996 under the symbol LCAV.

In a crowning transaction in 1997, LCAV used its common stock to purchase Refractive Centers International, a subsidiary of Summit Technology (Nasdaq NMS: BEAM). In the deal, LCAV issued 17 million shares of common stock and in return got Summit's 19 wholly owned and operated refractive surgery centers around the country. Of the 17 million shares issued to Summit, 9 million were redistributed to Summit shareholders and significantly broadened LCAV's shareholder base. As an added sweetener, the subsidiary that LCAV bought had a cash balance of $10 million at the time of the closing.

Reverse mergers such as LCAVs have many advantages:

◆ **They are impervious to market conditions.** Conventional IPOs derive a lot of their drama and tension from market conditions. That is, if the market is in a slump, the underwriter may pull the plug on the deal. Or, if an IPO candidate is in an industry that's making unfavorable headlines, investors may shy away from the deal, causing it to implode. Not so with a reverse merger. The deal hinges on whether or not the people who control the shell believe in the operating private company and want to be acquired by it. Market conditions have little to do with the initial transaction.

◆ **They have a short timetable.** A traditional public offering can drag on for months, sometimes more than a year. Unfortunately, the time it takes to do the deal is one of the most critical periods in a company's life. The prolonged distraction of an IPO, which often happens while the owners are trying to make the transition from an entrepreneurial organization to a professional one, can have disastrous effects and even nullify the growth upon which the offering is predicated. In addition, during the many months it takes to put together an IPO, market conditions can deteriorate, closing the company's window of opportunity. By contrast (circumstances permitting) a reverse merger can be completed in as little as 45 days.

◆ **They cost less.** By most estimates, a traditional IPO requires a company to ante up at least $200,000 in legal, audit, and printing fees just to get a preliminary prospectus on the street. To drive the deal to a close, the costs go even higher. A reverse merger, on the other hand, can be completed for $60,000 to $100,000, according to Art Beroff, a New York–based expert on reverse mergers and the architect of the LCAV deal.

◆ **They bring increased financing options.** Entrepreneurs should consider a reverse merger in order to increase their options for raising additional capital. One such option is a private offering. According to financier Beroff, perhaps the greatest impediment small, private companies face when they are trying to raise capital is the liquidity issue. "If investors like a company, they tend to believe it will succeed," says Beroff. "But their biggest fear is, even if the company does succeed, how will they get their investment back?"

Smart investors know that even a successful company may not be able to go public if the market conditions are unfavorable. However, for a company that is already public, the likelihood of developing a market for its common stock that accurately values the company and allows the investors to sell their shares is much better. For this reason, says Beroff, "Private investors are much more likely to invest in companies that are already public, as opposed to those that still have that hurdle to leap."

Another financing option is the issuance and exercise of warrants. These are similar to options, giving the holder the right to purchase additional shares in a company at predetermined prices. When many warrant holders exercise their option to purchase additional shares, the company receives an influx of capital, as shown in the diagram at right.

The exercise of warrants can be quick and easy, but it's

Theoretical Warrant Exercise

| PUBLIC COMPANY | ① ② ③ | PUBLIC INVESTORS HOLDING WARRANTS |

1 Exercise Right to Purchase 500,000 Additional Shares of Stock @ $5.00/Share
2 Remittance of $2.5 Million
3 Issuance of Stock Certificates for 500,000 Common Shares

not for everyone. Issuing additional shares may require a registration statement with the Securities and Exchange Commission (SEC)—precisely the expensive and time-consuming task that many companies are seeking to avoid with a reverse merger. Additionally, the exercise of warrants almost always requires the assistance of a brokerage firm. Finding the right firm can take a lot of time. More important, brokerage firms rarely cause warrants to be exercised according to the above model, but instead use a technique described below.

For some companies, the shortcomings of a reverse merger are negligible. For others, the problems are insurmountable, making a reverse merger an inappropriate financing strategy.

The following are some of the plan's disadvantages:

◆ **Poor image.** Over the years, reverse mergers have gained their share of controversy. It is easy to see why. To start with, the technique frequently relies upon recycling a failed company. For instance, STN, Inc., the leading long-distance reseller in Canada when that market was deregulated at the beginning of the decade, was actively traded on Nasdaq as a promising up-and-comer. However, STN became public through a reverse merger with Rawhide International, a dormant natural-resources company trading on Canada's Alberta Stock Exchange—not the kind of pedigree that made Wall Street analysts and investors eager for the company's stock.

◆ **Controversial exercise of warrants.** The poor image of reverse mergers is exacerbated by the way in which warrants are often exercised on their behalf. Firms that complete a reverse merger and hire a brokerage firm to exercise their warrants often see the process executed as shown below:

The problem is that at the end of the day, public investors are holding stock they purchased for $7 per share. Note also that the broker took in $3.5 million, but contractually only had to remit $2.5 million to the company. The broker made $1 million, less what it cost the firm to purchase the warrants. The company is capitalized, yes, but the broker's pockets have

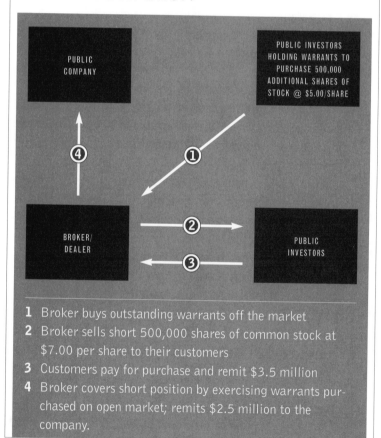

Warrant Exercise when Brokers Sell Short

PUBLIC COMPANY

PUBLIC INVESTORS HOLDING WARRANTS TO PURCHASE 500,000 ADDITIONAL SHARES OF STOCK @ $5.00/SHARE

④ ①

BROKER/ DEALER

②

③

PUBLIC INVESTORS

1 Broker buys outstanding warrants off the market
2 Broker sells short 500,000 shares of common stock at $7.00 per share to their customers
3 Customers pay for purchase and remit $3.5 million
4 Broker covers short position by exercising warrants purchased on open market; remits $2.5 million to the company.

been handsomely lined by public investors now holding expensive stock; management is under enormous pressure to make the company worth what investors paid for it.

All of this maneuvering is made possible by the unfortunate fact that, with the issue trading thinly, it's easy to create an arbitrage between the price of the common stock and the exercise price of the underlying warrants. The many implosions that have occurred on the heels of such financings have tarnished the reputation of reverse mergers.

◆ **Interaction with new shareholders.** In most cases, a reverse merger transaction leaves companies with a shareholder base that new management does not know. These shareholders can cause difficulties by continually selling their shares as a new trading market develops. In addition, creditors and other parties injured by the predecessor company can step forward and make claims. Unfortunately, when there are new operating assets in the company, the incentive to make these claims is increased.

◆ **Capital still must be raised.** Reverse mergers are not an end in themselves but a way to enable a company to raise money by some other transaction. Though this technique is theoretically quick and easy, there are, as with any securities transaction, enough land mines to make the process long and complex. In most instances, just doing the deal is the halfway point in the race. When it's done, capital still has to be raised.

As a case in point, consider San Diego–based PMR Corp., which merged in 1988 with Zaron Capital Corp., a shell company. PMR develops and manages psychiatric programs for hospitals. Though Zaron was a "clean" shell with no predecessor entities, the original reverse merger transaction took nearly a year. When the deal was done, PMR didn't have any more capital than when it started the process. However, the wait was worth it. PMR quickly raised additional capital, and the company, which now trades on the Nasdaq exchange, was the highest percentage gainer on the American Stock Exchange (ASE) in 1996, returning more than 450 percent to investors during the year.

◆ **Difficulty in developing a market.** Even though an exciting, private company merges with a public company, it doesn't mean the markets will take notice. Continental American Transportation, near Atlanta, Georgia, merged with a shell corporation; through a series of acquisitions it became one of the 20 largest trucking companies in the United States. Nonetheless, trading remained erratic, with the common stock barely responding to the underlying growth engineered by the new management team.

GETTING STARTED WITH A REVERSE MERGER

IF, DESPITE THE CHALLENGES, YOU STILL WANT TO PURSUE A reverse merger, the first task is to find a shell. The sources are fairly predictable. Ask an attorney. Every metropolitan area—even if it's not a financial hub—has a law firm with an active corporate securities practice. More than likely, the firm has a dormant public company sitting on its shelves. If it doesn't, the firm probably has worked recently on a case that resulted in the decline of a public company. Though it never hurts, you do not need a warm-body introduction to call a securities lawyer about a shell corporation. Securities lawyers are obligated to field such overtures because, dormant or not, it is in the best interest of the public company they represent to respond to inquiries that could have an influence on shareholder value.

An equally likely alternative is an accountant. Anyone who controls a dormant public company knows its value, and as a result, keeps its financial statements, such as they are, current. If the shell is a "reporting" company—meaning it makes quarterly and annual filings as per the Securities and Exchange Act of 1934—then its financial statements must be audited. In either event, a good accountant can lead you to shell companies.

Next, you must devise a financing strategy. Remember, the reverse merger is an indirect route to raising capital. You need to consider how creating a public company can be utilized to bring capital in the front door.

If a warrant exercise seems appropriate, then you want to find a merger candidate that not only has warrants outstanding, but also has registered the underlying shares with the

SEC. Companies that want to raise capital by exercising warrants, despite the potential pitfalls, must find a brokerage firm to assist with the transaction.

If a private offering will be sold after the company becomes public (i.e., a private placement) then the reverse merger must be very carefully structured. Specifically, the amount of "loose stock"—stock owned by investors that the new owners do not know and cannot influence—must be minimized so that a stable bid and ask quote can be established. One way to accomplish this is to recapitalize the company in such a way that the percentage stake held by public shareholders is reduced to a minority stake of 10 percent or less. Recapitalizing in this way is bound to create some ill will among shareholders who are still paying attention. On the plus side, however, reducing the impact of their potential sell orders makes for a more stable trading market. And once a stable bid and ask price are established, investors can be more easily enticed to buy shares privately at a discount to the market.

For example, if the quote on the stock is $5, private investors are offered the opportunity to purchase common stock at $3. This incentive will disappear, however, if sell orders from other investors flood the market, and the price of the common stock dips down to $2. It's not that any smart investor is going to think he can buy common stock in a private transaction for $3 and then sell it on the open market at the $5 bid. It is simply easier to sell a private deal where there is some immediate upside to point to, and a clearly defined exit strategy for the investor if the company prospers.

Finally, entrepreneurs interested in a reverse merger should budget time and effort to elevate the company's image. Dr. Joffe, chairman of LCA-Vision, who used the reverse merger technique to such brilliant results, said that although it was the right path for his company, "there's definitely a stigma attached to them." He believes this is largely because the process is misunderstood.

Entrepreneurs can, however, take steps to elevate the profile of their deal. They can hire a Big Six accounting firm.

Nothing inspires confidence more than an opinion from one of the national firms. They can also hire a white-shoe law firm. While most financial professionals and intermediaries believe that lawyers are sharks, they still prefer to swim with the better ones.

Some other steps: Look for merger candidates that do not have any previous incarnations. If a public company has failed operations in its recent (or even distant) past, some of the tarnish can rub off on you.

And finally, don't be greedy. Many reverse mergers are structured so that at the end of the deal, the public owns as little as 5 percent of the company. Unfortunately, there's almost no incentive for other investors to get involved if the only people who truly benefit are the insiders. If you are going to get the public involved with the hope of forging a truly symbiotic relationship, leave some value on the table.

In many ways the rap against reverse mergers is akin to the knock made against junk bonds during the 1980s. Sure, junk was used by corporate raiders to buy companies and break them up, giving the bonds a bad reputation. But junk bonds also nurtured a generation of exciting growth companies like Medco Containment, Calvin Klein, and Hovnanian, that prior to the advent of junk had no access to the bond market because they lacked an investment grade rating.

Like junk bonds, reverse mergers are simply a technique. In the final analysis, the character of the technique depends on the character of the people behind the deal.

Exempt Public Offerings

ONE OF THE SERIOUS IMPEDIMENTS TO AN IPO IS THE registration statement that companies must file with the SEC, which requires, among other things, a set of audited financial statements. It is time consuming and difficult. And it's expensive in more ways than one. According to Sandy Robertson, of BancAmerica Robertson Stephens, "A conventional IPO takes 25 percent of a president's time and 50 percent of a chief financial officer's time during the year they file and go public."

Fortunately, small public offerings of $1 million or less can be exempt from registration. Specifically, Rule 504 of Regulation D of the Securities Act of 1934 offers this exemption. In addition, most states offer exemptions from state securities laws for small public offerings. By structuring deals to take advantage of exemptions at both the federal and state level, companies gain direct access to public investors while avoiding many of the barriers associated with IPOs.

If the offering is done correctly, the shares can trade on Nasdaq's Bulletin Board stock market. Although the Bulletin Board is one of the lowest tiers of the Nasdaq market, it still offers quote and trading information on terminals around the world. As with the reverse merger, the creation of a public vehicle has almost incalculable value and can dramatically ease the process of raising additional capital.

To see this technique in action, consider the case of Twilight Productions, a tiny independent film producer in Hollywood, California. With several years of filmmaking experience under his belt, Eric Galler wanted to make films for the obscure but thriving low-budget segment of the market. Rather than going to Wall Street, Galler raised approximately $60,000 for his company through an exempt offering by selling units of common stock and warrants to investors. The warrants gave the holders the right to purchase additional shares at predetermined prices. With this funding, Twilight was able to produce its first film.

Although the initial offering was small, it was still significant because the company was able to list its shares on the Bulletin Board, under the symbol TWIP. Now, with the rudiments of a trading market for its shares in place, Twilight was able to raise additional growth capital by causing its warrants to be exercised. Through this effort, Twilight received an additional $900,000. Galler says the structure of the offering was successful. "We were able to raise start-up funds inexpensively," he says, "and as we proved our concept, we were able to take advantage of the trading market to raise additional funds."

Exempt public offerings have significant advantages:

◆ **Easier financial reporting.** Exempt offerings do not

require audited financial statements. This is important because audited financials, which are de rigueur for IPOs as well as some exempt offerings, add no less than $25,000 to the cost of raising funds, and in some cases add *several hundred thousand* dollars.

◆ **Speedier transactions.** By removing the need to complete a federal registration statement, companies can raise funds much faster. At the federal level, companies need only complete a fill-in-the-blanks form, popularly referred to as Form D. At the state level, things can get a little more complicated. Some states require detailed filings, while others require a simple notification that can be completed in minutes.

◆ **Lower costs.** As mentioned earlier, the absence of audited financial statements reduces accounting costs. In the same vein, the absence of a complex registration statement reduces legal fees. All totaled, the costs for Twilight's $960,000 financing were in the neighborhood of $20,000.

◆ **Gateway to upper tiers of the Nasdaq stock market.** Exempt offerings can trade on the Nasdaq Bulletin Board with relative ease. However, if a company grows and meets certain quantitative requirements, it can "graduate" to the small-cap or national market tiers of the market.

NATURALLY, EXEMPT OFFERINGS HAVE CERTAIN DISADVANtages, as well:

◆ **Limited size.** The 504 offerings discussed here are limited to raising $1 million in any 12-month period. For some companies, such as restaurants, $750,000 is all the equity capital they may ever need. For others, such as pharmaceutical development companies, $1 million does not even make a dent in the amount of capital they need.

◆ **Limited state exemptions.** Although states offer exemptions from their securities laws, these exemptions can be limiting to the point of uselessness. For instance, in Ohio exempt offerings can be sold to no more than 10 investors. In most states, companies that need to sell to more than the decreed number of investors will find they have to register, which may involve drafting a prospectus, or filing a Form U-7.

Form U-7 is also known as a SCOR (Small Company Offering Registration) form. Although SCOR deals represent an advance in equity capital formation for small businesses and a quantum leap in unifying the myriad state regulations into one filing, it's no day at the beach. In fact, when all 50 questions of Form U-7 are answered, the end result, known as an *offering circular*, looks suspiciously like a federal registration statement, which is the time-consuming and complicated paperwork that most small businesses seek to avoid. In addition, many states add suitability requirements to an offering that dictate minimum net worth requirements for investors.

Testimony to the degree of difficulty associated with traditional SCOR offerings comes from the large numbers of companies that never make it through the process. According to Tom Stewart-Gordon, publisher of the *SCOR Report*, 65 to 70 percent of companies that try a SCOR deal fail. And, he says, that doesn't include the untold numbers who attempt the filing but never complete it because of the complexity or the legal or accounting costs involved.

INITIAL STEPS TO A 504 OFFERING

IF YOU DECIDE TO RAISE MONEY, THERE ARE LOTS OF WAYS TO approach and complete a 504 offering. Described below is a methodology that takes maximum advantage of federal and state exemptions and the ability to create a public vehicle on the Bulletin Board stock market. Clearly, however, each company's circumstances and requirements differ:

♦ **Structure your deal.** How much capital do you want to raise and what percentage of the company will it represent? Entrepreneurs contemplating a 504 offering must come up with fast answers about what their business is worth *(see Chapter 7 for an analysis of how to value your business)* and, as a consequence, how much of it they must sell to get the capital they need. Whereas the reverse merger, as an intermediate step to financing, does not always provoke hard questions about valuation, a 504 deal, with the immediate prospect of selling securities to investors, does.

♦ **Hire a securities attorney with experience in exempt**

public offerings. Although the exemptions from federal and state securities laws are meant to simplify the process, no securities transaction is ever simple. Don't attempt the process without experienced securities counsel.

◆ **Line up a brokerage firm.** To create a trading mechanism on the Nasdaq's Bulletin Board, two brokerage firms must elect to make a market in your company's stock by filing certain forms with the National Association of Securities Dealers (NASD). For most brokers, market making in unregistered securities is not the kind of business they want. They make little money on the deal, and they perceive that regulatory risks exist. The best bet is a referral from a lawyer or a small local brokerage firm that can get to know you and your business.

◆ **Sell shares in New York; Florida; Washington, D.C.; and Colorado first.** These states do not restrict the resale of shares by individual investors. This feature is critical because it allows unrestricted trading to occur on the Bulletin Board.

Obviously for many companies and entrepreneurs, this is a difficult tactic. One strategy for overcoming the challenge is to raise just a small amount of capital in these states—perhaps as little as $25,000—and use the existence of these sales to establish a quotation on the Bulletin Board. Then, use the power of having a public company to raise capital with investors closer to home in a private, intrastate offering, which takes advantage of exemptions from state securities laws.

Sound convoluted? Perhaps. But not nearly as convoluted as satisfying the requirements of some state securities regulators. Jim Smith, founder of what was once Triex Group International, a specialty lighting company in San Leandro, California, spent almost $100,000 in legal, accounting, and printing fees getting a never-completed SCOR offering registered to the satisfaction of the state's securities regulators during 1995. "That whole episode was a period in my life that I would rather not remember," he says.

◆ **Purchase coverage in *Corporation Records*, published by Standard & Poor's Corp.** Once the issue is trading on a recognized stock market such as the Bulletin Board, investors in almost all states can purchase shares—not from the company, but in a secondary market—provided there is detailed information on the company that is generally available to the public. *Corporation Records*, because of its wide distribution and its role as the primary source of information for many investment databases and quotation services, adequately fulfills this role in the eyes of some 40 state regulators.

The ability of investors to buy and sell shares nationally doesn't put any capital in the company's coffers per se. It simply makes the process of raising additional funds as a company grows much, much easier.

One business that profited handsomely from an exempt offering was Electric Car Battery Company, of Solana Beach, California. The company developed a new battery, which inventor George Carlsen thought might win market share among electric vehicles used on golf courses and in retirement communities. When Electric Car needed capital to finish development and fund a commercial rollout of the product, it chose to do a 504 offering, says Don Hutton, the company's chief financial officer. "It seemed to be the most straightforward path to the capital we needed," he says.

Initially, the company raised $200,000 by selling 100,000 units, consisting of common stock and warrants, at $2 per unit. The company used a broker to help sell the units to investors in New York; Washington, D.C.; Colorado; and Florida. The deal was completed during the third quarter of 1997, and Hutton says the company will use the funds to finish product development and will enter the market during the fourth quarter. During this time period, Hutton will also work to get shares of Electric Car trading on the Bulletin Board.

"The thinking behind our strategy," says Hutton, "is that the combination of starting product sales in a thriving market, with some kind of trading or resale mechanism, will make the job of raising the additional funds much easier than if we were strictly a private company."

Direct Public Offerings

THE PRIMARY DIFFERENCE BETWEEN DIRECT PUBLIC OFFERINGS (DPOs) and reverse mergers or exempt public offerings is, to a degree, philosophical. The underlying idea of reverse mergers and exempt public offerings is to first create a *public* vehicle that in turn will increase financing options. By contrast, the underlying idea of a DPO is to raise capital from a company's natural affinity groups, such as customers, suppliers, and members of the surrounding community—with little or no concern for whether or not there is a trading market.

Michael Quinn used a DPO to raise money for his small pharmaceutical company. After 10 years in business, Quinn wanted to go national. However, his Hahnemann Laboratories, Inc., of San Rafael, California, a manufacturer of homeopathic medicines, needed to become an FDA-licensed pharmaceutical manufacturer if it was going to actively market its product across state lines. Where would Quinn get the capital to outfit a new facility?

"I went to a commercial bank, and they said, 'No way,'" recalls Quinn. Investment bankers weren't offering much comfort either. However, Quinn had an epiphany when he realized that if just 200 of his more than 28,000 customers each invested about $2,000, his company would have the equity capital it needed. Intrigued by the prospect and given little hope from conventional sources of capital, Quinn marketed common shares himself in a $467,000 DPO.

Quinn sent out more than 35,000 offering announcements. Typically, people interested in alternative medicine are not those usually interested in the stock market, says Quinn. His deal—in a way, an alternative public offering—seemed to have a unique appeal to these investors. The announcements resulted in about 1,700 requests for prospectuses. There were another 400 requests for prospectuses from friends, family, associates, and colleagues. Of the initial 2,100 investors who received a prospectus, Quinn says that about 240 ultimately invested.

None of this work was quick or easy. Quinn started drafting his prospectus in July 1994; twelve months later, in August 1995, he closed his deal's $430,000 minimum. Of his 240 investors, Quinn estimates that just 15 percent, or 36 investors, sent in a check after reading the prospectus. To get the other 200 or so, Quinn had to dial for dollars. In all, he figures that he talked to between 700 and 800 investors on the telephone. Nor was any of this cheap. Legal, audit, printing, and marketing costs totaled $102,000, says Quinn.

Although the entire effort took valuable time and resources away from the business, Quinn says it was not without benefits above and beyond raising the money. "Sure, there were days when I wished I would run into just one person who had $500,000." However, there was a tremendous benefit to talking to so many customers and finding out what their needs and attitudes were. "Reaching out to so many people and telling your story is never bad for a business, if it's done with the right kind of heart and attitude," he says.

In fact, sales jumped while Quinn was most preoccupied with selling the deal. They reached $691,000 during Hahnemann's fiscal year 1996 (ending June 30, 1996)—about $100,000 higher than the previous year. The momentum has spilled into fiscal 1997, with sales of some $400,000 at midyear.

Quinn has not been concerned with aftermarket trading. He has left that to a stockbroker who keeps a "book," matching buyers and sellers. Most of the investors are holding onto their shares, says Quinn. Upside potential seems to be the reason. "It would be nearly impossible for one of the major pharmaceutical companies to grow 10 times bigger," he says. "But we definitely can."

Direct offerings are time consuming for an executive who is otherwise engaged in running a company. Drew Field, an attorney, consultant, and author of *Direct Public Offerings*, says that such an offering is no less complex or challenging than an offering done by an underwriter. "But it is a more manageable way to go," he says. In a direct offering, entrepreneurs do not have to accommodate or rely upon investment bankers, which can prove difficult and dangerous.

"You can manage a direct public offering just like you would any other project," he says.

However, he counsels, this financing option has its limitations:

♦ **Absence of liquidity.** Companies that in addition to raising capital must provide an immediate exit for early investors, or an accurate valuation of the company for estate planning purposes, will find that direct offerings fall short in helping them reach their ultimate objectives.

♦ **The company's stock has little value as currency to acquire other companies.** Without a trading market, there is little reason, except a great deal of faith, for someone to accept a company's stock in lieu of cash.

♦ **Little opportunity for entrepreneurs to realize gains.** It would be all but unheard of for the founder of a company to sell his or her shares to investors in a DPO. In addition, with no active trading market, there's little hope of selling them on the market after the deal is done.

In summary, DPOs provide a solution for companies that, in the next three to five years, need patient equity capital and not much else. Once the needs start to extend beyond this, the effectiveness of this approach becomes compromised. In truth, this is all most companies need, even though many entrepreneurs become romanced by the idea of a full-blown IPO. Maintaining an active aftermarket, one of the chief burdens of an IPO, is precisely what causes many entrepreneurs to run their company into the ground.

NOT EVERY COMPANY IS A GOOD CANDIDATE FOR A DIRECT offering. Field provides the following criteria:

♦ **The business is easy to understand.** Individuals who participate in direct offerings tend not to purchase shares in companies they do not understand. Because they are individuals, the scope of what they understand is much narrower than brokerages or institutions with access to research departments.

♦ **The company is established and profitable.** The direct-offering process involves little direct selling, but a lot of reading and evaluation on the part of would-be shareholders. As a result, these offerings tend to attract investors who are more cautious than speculative.

♦ **The company has natural affinity groups.** Customers, clients, and the community may have an affinity for the company. It's through this relationship that much of the direct offering will be sold. One of the fundamental questions entrepreneurs face in this regard is whether or not the affinity they perceive is mutual and strong enough to motivate prospective investors to consider their offering. In addition, for offerings to succeed entrepreneurs must be able to uncover the names, telephone numbers, and addresses of people who have a natural affinity for their company.

Based on these criteria, a lot of companies are candidates for a direct offering; however, some clearly are not. For instance, a manufacturer of stained-glass windows for homes is a likely candidate. A biotechnology company at the R&D stage is not. An agricultural cooperative is a candidate for a DPO; a manufacturer of industrial abrasives may not be. A lawn-care company is a good prospect; a business that operates prisons for government entities is probably not.

FROM A REGULATORY PERSPECTIVE, DPOS CAN BE CONDUCTED in accordance with the same securities laws that regulate conventional IPOs, or they can be conducted within the context of exemptions that are offered by states and the federal government. The scale from hardest to easiest is offered below:

1 **Full registration.** Companies seeking to raise more than $5 million and also wanting to trade on a stock exchange or the top two tiers of the Nasdaq stock market (though this is highly unlikely without a brokerage firm leading the charge), must file a registration statement with the SEC. This is a major undertaking for any company, which is made both more difficult and easier by the absence of an investment banker in the direct-offering process. It's more difficult because investment bankers have vast experience shepherding these registrations through the SEC. However, it's easier because the company can make changes to the registration statement in response to SEC "comments" without worry-

ing about how the investment banker will react.

2 **Regulation A filings.** Companies that want to raise more than $1 million but less than $5 million can take advantage of the exemption from federal registration by filing under what is known as Regulation A of the Securities Act of 1933. While the feds do not require audited financial statements in a Regulation A filing, some states do.

3 **SCOR offerings.** Companies that want to raise less than $1 million in a DPO may take advantage of the Small Company Offering Registration, popularly known as SCOR. It is accepted in 46 states and the District of Columbia and requires almost no filings with the SEC; the form is not accepted in Alabama, Delaware, Nebraska, or Hawaii. The SCOR form, also known as Form U-7, is, as discussed above, complex and challenging.

4 **Federal and state exemptions.** Companies that want to avoid all filings can, at the federal level, take advantage of the exemption offered by Regulation D, and at the state level, structure their offerings to qualify for a particular state or states exemption. In most cases, this means selling securities to no more than a specified number of investors, usually from five to 35, as well as foregoing advertising and solicitation.

If a direct offering still sounds good, evaluate your ability to pull it off. The direct offering process takes time to execute. In addition, it requires leadership. Entrepreneurs must honestly consider if they have enough of both to see the process through. Remember that Michael Quinn at Hahnemann Labs talked to more than 700 potential investors in the course of finishing his DPO.

As a final word of advice, DPOs don't work well without a large group of investors who have some sort of connection with the company, its product, or its service. Some companies, such as publishing concerns, have a large base of customers and enough information about them to easily launch a direct marketing effort. Other companies, such as restaurants, also have a large base of customers but typically know little about them.

For companies such as this, the question becomes: "Can I

buy lists of my customers or potential customers, and would these lists be effective?" In the case of a restaurant, yes, lists of restaurant customers can be bought. Unfortunately, the affinity those people have for *your* company, simply because it operates a restaurant, is not strong enough to merit soliciting them for investment capital. On the other end of the spectrum, however, an environmental-services company can rent membership lists of environmental groups, associations, and institutions; a company making home-care products can rent the membership list of the Visiting Nurse Association; and a company making body-building products can get the names of consumers who read *Fitness* magazine.

For a complete guide to the DPO process, buy *Direct Public Offerings*, by Drew Field. It offers the most comprehensive information on structuring a DPO, from assembling the team of professionals to launching a direct marketing effort (Sourcebooks Inc., 121 North Washington Street, Naperville, Il 60540; 800-432-7444).

The Limitations of Cyberspace

ENTREPRENEURS AND FINANCIERS ARE BEGINNING TO FEEL the impact of the Internet on the process of raising money for early-stage companies. One day, the Internet may well be the best tool for entrepreneurs intent on raising the capital they need to grow their businesses.

But not yet. William Wetzel, professor emeritus of the University of New Hampshire's Whittemore School of Business, and founder of the Center for Venture Economics, says, "It is not, at the close of 1997, likely that companies will raise capital over the Internet." At this point, it's certainly not easier than the conventional ways of attracting capital.

At present, raising money on the Internet is somewhere beyond the novelty stage but not quite at the utility stage. If anything, the ability to raise money over the Internet has been hyped to the point where it is misleading. To understand why this is so, witness the experience of Andrew Klein, a securities attorney turned brewer, turned investment banker.

The story dates back to late 1992 when Klein, then with the law firm Cravath, Swain & Moore in New York City, took a few months off to travel. While in Holland, Klein tried some so-called wit beer, which is brewed with wheat and spiced with orange. When he learned that wit beer wasn't available anywhere outside of Belgium or Holland, Klein sensed an opportunity.

It knocked on his door several months later, back in the United States, Klein received a phone call from a Dutch brewer who had cashed out on the sale of his company. Was Klein interested in teaming up to brew wit beer in the United States? By January 1993, just six months after his summer sabbatical, Klein had left his law firm (with commitments from 13 partners to invest) and established Spring Street Brewery, located in Manhattan.

Klein feels he initially had all the luck an entrepreneur could hope for. Local bars could not get enough of his wit beer, there was lots of media hoopla, and distributors from across the country were offering to sell the product. "But when opportunity knocks," says Klein, "it usually wants money. Our initial $800,000 of capital, which seemed like a lot when we started, quickly turned into a grossly inadequate amount."

In the fall of 1993, Klein set out to raise between $2 million and $3 million from angels and venture capitalists. While the process was encouraging, it was too drawn out for Klein, with every investor or fund sending him away with new questions to research.

Realizing he needed an efficient mechanism to raise lots of money on a continuous basis, Klein decided to sell stock directly to the public. He knew that ice-cream maker Ben & Jerry's had initially sold stock to the public by advertising their deal on product packaging. Klein struck upon another idea that promised wide exposure: put the prospectus on the Internet and open the company up to millions of potential investors.

The mechanics of Klein's revolution were basic. Spring Street Brewery simply put the prospectus for its offering on the company's Web site (**www.witbeer.com**). Investors could visit the site, learn about the company, download subscription documents, and, if they were interested in investing, send a check to Spring Street.

Because it was the first-ever deal of its kind, Klein's single press release about an Internet IPO brought with it a windfall of publicity in the national news media. With the publicity came hits on the Web site—some 500,000 of them. Initially, the pace was furious, and Klein recalls receiving as much as $85,000 a week. By the end of 1995, Spring Street Brewery raised $1.6 million from 3,500 investors over the course of 10 months.

While the SEC quickly and easily gave its approval to Klein to post his prospectus and other offering documentation on the Internet, the regulators were not at all pleased when Klein designed a series of bulletin boards that would allow shareholders to trade Spring Street common stock among themselves. After news of Spring Street's Internet trading hit the national business media—which had a field day with the story line of established stock markets being bypassed—Klein soon found himself on a conference call with 11 SEC attorneys.

After reviewing the situation, the SEC ultimately allowed Spring Street to continue to operate its Internet trading service, but under conditions that for Klein and Spring Street carried too much liability. Rather than cave, and in the true spirit of an entrepreneur, Klein formed Wit Capital as an investment banking firm to use the power of the Internet to raise money for emerging companies, particularly those concentrating on new media and Internet content.

When the history books are written, there will surely be a place in them for Andrew Klein, as the visionary entrepreneur who first tapped the power of the Internet to fund his fledgling brewery.

Visionaries, however, have an advantage that none of their followers enjoy: *They are first*. In the case of Spring Street, being the first "Internet IPO" created what bordered on a self-fulfilling prophecy because the Spring Street story was carried by nearly every national print and broadcast media.

Today, however, companies can't generate the kind of publicity that Spring Street earned. Entrepreneurs now looking to raise money on the Internet come face-to-face with the reality that while the Internet offers a potent medium for distributing information to potential investors, it offers almost no mechanism for selling to them.

What is left, therefore, is hope. Specifically, entrepreneurs raising money on the Internet hope that:

1 Investors find the Web site where the offering is posted.
2 Investors are intrigued enough to download the offering circular, memorandum or prospectus, and subscription documents.
3 Investors who do this reside in a state where the offering can be sold.
4 Investors print out, carefully review the documents, and are simultaneously excited and comforted by what they read.
5 Investors on the Internet who now have access to delicate company information, including the compensation data and the company's financial statements, do not use this information against the entrepreneur.
6 Investors will respond to further entreaties from the company by sending in a check.
7 If they are not so well organized, they hope investors take it upon themselves to mail a check to the company's escrow agent.
8 Enough investors do this that the "minimum" on the offering can be closed—and that enough additional investors come aboard that the rest of the offering can be closed.
9 That all of this happens quickly.

THE BEST ADVICE? IF YOU ARE DOING A DPO OR AN EXEMPT offering, use the power of the Internet to distribute information to investors, but do not rely upon it to lead you to capital.

CHAPTER 5

Venture Capital

ENTURE CAPITAL IS WONDERFUL STUFF.

Much of the nation's wealth was created in no small part by venture capital firms. The development of the semiconductor was financed by venture capitalists. From this came minicomputers, also funded by venture capitalists. Then came the personal computer, financed as well by venture capitalists. The personal computer spawned industries in software, peripherals, and the networking equipment that linked them. All of these industries were financed by venture capitalists. Entrepreneurs made billions. Venture capitalists made billions.

However, the influence didn't stop there. Venture capitalists shifted the tectonic plates beneath Wall Street and made brokers, institutional investors, and investment bankers pay attention to, and finance, tiny technology companies. With the liquidity of the public equity markets, the wealth spread to institutions, mutual funds, employees with employee stock ownership plan (ESOP) holdings, and individual investors. An investor who purchased 1,000 shares of Microsoft common stock in the company's 1986 initial public offering (IPO) for $21,000, now has 36,000 shares worth about $5 million.

These benefits come with a price; the price is *selectivity*. Consider some of the numbers involved. Dun and Bradstreet reports 600,000 to 700,000 new incorporations each year. By contrast, a 1995 survey conducted by Price Waterhouse for the National Venture Capital Association (NVCA) found that venture firms comprising the NVCA invested about $7.5 billion in 1,586 deals that year. Comparing the two numbers suggests that venture capital funds are financing 0.2 percent of the new businesses created each year. It also means that 99.8 percent of American businesses had to go somewhere else to find equity capital.

Is your company part of the 0.2 percent, or is it part of the other 99.8 percent that must look elsewhere? To find out, take the following test:

1 **Is yours a technology company?** About 80 percent of a venture capitalist's portfolio is in technology. It's not that venture capitalists don't fund low- or no-tech companies. They do; just not that often. The reasoning goes: If your company is not technology driven, it's behind the eight ball to begin with. In addition, the competition among nontechnology companies for the few institutional venture capital dollars that are available is even keener, meaning that if your company is low- or no-tech, it's got to be a truly spectacular performer. Why the relentless (and sometimes enervating) focus on technology? The answer to this question may lie in the answer to the next one.

2 **Is your company capable of being a market leader?** Venture capitalists rarely finance a company that is going up against a market leader with a similar product or service. Why? It's too difficult and expensive to succeed simply by stealing share from a well-entrenched and larger company. Not that a company cannot succeed in large markets with large competitors; just look at all the hamburger restaurants. However, few of them generate the kind of returns that venture capitalists require. This is why technology is so attractive to venture capitalists. Advances and breakthroughs can shatter the established paradigm of existing markets, or create vast new ones. Consider how Oracle's concept of network computers may challenge, and perhaps even shatter, Microsoft's grip on the market. Or consider how inventor Edwin Land's Polaroid camera used new technology to create a niche that his company dominated. With low-technology consumer products, such as injection-molded, plastic housewares, or ubiquitous services such as restaurants, it's difficult to change the rules of the game.

3 **Can your company be built inexpensively?** Inexpensive is a relative term. In a venture capitalist's nomenclature, that's

about $10 million or less. Sure, there are lots of companies that could make a billion dollars by, say, developing hydro-electric plants in China. The problem is they need $5 billion in investment capital.

4 **Does your company require a material amount of capital?** This is the flip side to inexpensively building a business. If a company needs just $500,000, for an institutional venture capitalist with $50 million to invest, it's usually a pass. The reason is cost. It takes a lot of time and money to research, negotiate, and monitor a deal. So, in order to deliver the kind of hands-on approach institutional venture capital investing requires, the venture capitalist would rather make 15 to 20 $2 million investments than 100 or so $500,000 investments.

5 **Can the company be acquired or go public?** The payday for venture capital investors comes when companies are sold or go public. If neither is likely to occur, venture capitalists won't be interested. It's not just a question of whether companies will generate the kind of performance that will allow them to be sold or go public. It's also a question of whether the founder is willing to go that route. If the business owner's posture is "I want to pass control and ownership of the business onto the next generation of my family," that generally stifles a venture capitalist's interest on the spot.

6 **Can the product or service generate gross margins of more than 50 percent?** For business owners who are trying to carve out a salary and a living, gross margins of 30 percent are fine. However, for venture capitalists who need to make a significant return, 30 percent margins are too thin. Not only is there little room for error but the prospects for an acquisition or an IPO, which are the big events for institutional venture capital investors, dim significantly.

7 **Can the company grow to $25 million in sales in five years, with the prospect of reaching $50 million to $100 million?** Eventually, it all gets back to the numbers. At $25 million in sales, a company just begins to generate the profits that make it worth enough that venture capitalists can get the kind of return they're looking for. Let's say, for instance, that a $25 million enterprise was bringing $5 million to the

bottom line—a feat, by the way, that is difficult to accomplish when the *gross* margin is 30 percent. If the company went public and was valued in the market at 20 times earnings, it would be worth $100 million. The venture capitalist who invested $10 million and owns 50 percent of the company now has a stake valued at $50 million, or five times the initial investment in five years—a middle-of-the-road target return for most venture capital funds.

John Martinson, who crafted the above diagnostic test, and a general partner with Edison Venture Funds of Lawrenceville, New Jersey, a venture capital firm with some $200 million under management, says, "If a company can't pass the last hurdle on sales and earnings growth, it should not waste its time pursuing institutional sources of venture capital."

More conservatively, a no to almost any of the preceding questions—with a possible but unlikely exception for the second and the sixth—makes the entire prospect of venture capital dim, at best. If you don't qualify for venture capital, don't waste your time looking. If you do qualify, however, then by all means start looking. As the chart below indicates, the supply of venture capital continues to rise.

However, don't let the amount of money that has been raised lull you into thinking that your search is going to be made easier by the increasing supply. More and more com-

Total Capital Raised by Institutional Venture Capital Funds by Year

YEAR	AMOUNT RAISED ($ BILLIONS)
1990	1.8
1991	1.3
1992	2.5
1993	2.5
1994	3.8
1995	4.4
1996	5.2

SOURCE: VENTURE ECONOMICS INVESTOR SERVICES

panies are seeking venture funding. However, far more challenging is the fact that companies already in a venture capitalist's portfolio demand more and more capital to reach fruition. Supplicants must compete with the companies that have already been financed.

In addition, do not be misled into thinking the appropriate response to a growing number of venture capital targets is sending a business plan to as many venture firms as possible. According to Glen Bierman, a managing director with Tycon Equity Partners, a venture capital and consulting firm in New York City, "Institutional venture capital firms tend to have fairly rigid investment criteria, which means there are, in truth, a limited number of deals that will interest any particular firm."

Therefore, says Bierman, it's much more effective to pick highly researched targets one by one than it is to send out as many business plans as possible and hope that one sticks. To paraphrase an old saying: When looking for venture capital, shoot with a rifle, not a shotgun.

Narrowing Your Search for Venture Capital

THE WAY TO NARROW YOUR SEARCH INTO THE MOST LIKELY pool of venture capital investors—assuming, of course, that your company qualifies in the first place—is to focus on only a few variables: leadership status, investment-size preference, stage of development, geography, industry preference, and, in some instances, amount of capital required.

◆ **Search by leadership status.** When searching for equity capital among angels, find a lead investor, a marquee personality who will bring other, more passive investors into the deal. "The same concept applies for institutional venture capital," says G. Jackson Tankersley, a general partner of the Centennial Funds, the largest venture capital pool in the Rocky Mountain region. "So much money has gone into this industry that there are now huge pools of capital that are essentially passive and invest alongside other venture firms." However, Tankersley adds, don't waste your time trying to get these more passive investors to invest directly in your deal.

In addition, Tankersley explains, "Large deals require a good lead investor who can make the job of syndicating the placement among several venture capital investors much easier. When it comes to raising $5 million or less, most large venture capital firms handle the financing internally. But for deals in excess of $5 million, many firms seek out other venture investors to participate.

◆ **Search by stage of development.** One of the most important criteria is the stage of development at which a venture capitalist will fund companies. Generally speaking, while venture capitalists will overcome distance and industry preferences for what he or she perceives to be a hot deal, they are generally quite rigid about a company's stage of development. One reason for this, according to David Freschman, president of the Delaware Innovation Fund, in Wilmington, Delaware, is that "while almost anybody can travel, not everyone can master investing in companies at every stage in their life cycle. There are huge differences between a company at the seed stage, versus one at the mezzanine stage."

The table at right shows the generally accepted stages of financing, along with corresponding company characteristics. The figure in the far right column represents the percentage of venture capitalists reporting a willingness to invest in companies at that stage of development. These percentages were developed from data in *Pratt's Guide to Venture Capital Sources,* published by Venture Economics, a division of Securities Data Company in Newark, New Jersey.

The bad news about searching out prospects by stage-of-development preference is that it eliminates a lot of potential leads. The good news is that eliminating so many firms prevents you from running down a lot of blind alleys. Says Delaware Innovation Fund's Freschman: "If you start cold calling venture capitalists who only invest in companies with revenues, and you're a year away from generating any, in most cases, you are wasting your precious time."

Parenthetically, the percentages shown on the chart at right provide more evidence regarding why venture capital is

Venture Investors by Stage

FINANCING	COMPANY CHARACTERISTICS	% VENTURE FIRMS REPORTING INTEREST
SEED FINANCING	Small amount of capital used to validate a business concept or technology	12.8
START-UP FINANCING	Generally ranges from $500,000 to as much as $3 million for companies that have completed product or service development and are now ready to commence initial marketing operations	13.6
FIRST-STAGE FINANCING	Generally ranges from $500,000 to $3 million. First-stage financing is for companies that successfully negotiated the start-up phase and are ready to commence full-scale manufacturing of a product or rollout of a service	17.5
SECOND-STAGE FINANCING	Generally ranges from $3 million to $8 million. Second-stage financing is for companies that are enjoying product or service acceptance and have growing working capital needs	23.2
MEZZANINE FINANCING	Ranges from $5 million to $12 million. Mezzanine financing is for companies that have demonstrated success and seek to expand the scope of their operations through new products, new services, new capacity, or intensified sales and marketing	32.7

so dear for early-stage companies. Only 13 percent of venture capitalists will look at companies with no revenues. Some 75 percent are looking for companies that are already successfully selling a product or service.

♦ **Search by investment-size preferences.** Another criterion, strongly related to stage-of-development preferences, is preferred investment size. A fund with $100 million under management probably does not want to make a $500,000 investment in your company. Why? To be fully invested by making $500,000 investments, the fund would have to finance 200 companies. That is too many to monitor. A fund of this size might prefer making investments in the neighborhood of $2 million to $6 million, instead.

According to Centennial's Tankersley, "Preference for a certain-sized investment is not always useful by itself, but when taken along with other criteria, can help in selecting venture capitalists who will most likely be interested in your company and its financing proposal."

♦ **Search by geography.** Playing the geography card can produce good results. There are several reasons for this, some related to the art and science of venture capital investing and some related to human nature.

First, most people have a bias for the hometown team. Second, most people do not like business travel. Therefore, situations closer to home have more appeal than ones 3,000 miles away. The third reason, and the most relevant to the proposition a venture capitalist offers a company, is related to value. Simply put, it's difficult for a venture capitalist to be a value-added investor when he or she is not even working in the same time zone as the company.

To discover the firms that are in your backyard, you first have to define it. Draw a ring around your company, representing a 150-mile radius; everything within the resulting circle is your backyard. For some folks in Montana, such an area may still *be* in their backyard, literally. There is hope, though: Some venture firms operate regionally. For instance, Seattle-based Cable & Howse Ventures looks at deals in the Northwest. Charlotte, North Carolina–based Kitty Hawk Capital looks at deals in the Southeast. And the Venture Capital

Fund of New England, located in Boston, looks at—no surprise here—deals in New England.

Also, consider that many states recognize the economic development potential of venture capital and finance pools of capital that invest in companies within their boundaries. To find a fund in your state, call or write the National Association of State Venture Funds, 301 NW 63rd Street, Oklahoma City, OK 73116; 405-848-8570.

◆ **Search by industry preference.** There is a direct relationship between an investor's time horizon and his knowledge of a company—its operations and industry. Security traders, who may own shares in a company for about 10 minutes, probably don't know who runs it, where it's located, or how many employees it has. Venture capitalists, on the other hand, with a five- to seven-year investment horizon, need to know everything about the companies in which they invest. Either because of this or to prepare for this, venture capitalists maintain industry preferences. These are certain businesses in which they prefer to invest, or in which they will invest exclusively. Industry preferences can be broad, such as computers and related equipment, or quite narrow, such as pollution control systems.

For entrepreneurs, this specialization can be a blessing. At the most basic level, in very narrowly defined niches, venture capitalists are more likely to talk to companies simply because they are interested in learning more about the companies in their industry. During these conversations, venture capitalists may provide additional, well-qualified leads, even if they are not interested in investing, .

Venture capitalists that specialize in an area are particularly valuable investors. According to Tankersley, "Other venture capitalists will acknowledge their expertise, and it will make your company a more attractive investment for later rounds of financing."

TO FIND THE DATA YOU WILL NEED TO CONDUCT A HIGHLY targeted search of venture capitalists, look at the following resources:

◆ *Pratt's Guide to Venture Capital Sources*, 40 West 57th

Street, New York, NY 10019; 212-830-9363. The guide, published by Securities Data Company, is offered in hardback and on CD-ROM, which makes searching by geographic preference, stage of development, and industry preference quick and easy.

◆ Another good source is VentureOne in San Francisco, which offers custom searches of its venture capital database based on key criteria. In addition, VentureOne publishes *Venture-Focus Reports*, which provides lists of top venture capitalists, contact information, and aggregate valuations by industry group. Write to: VentureOne, 590 Fulsom, San Francisco, CA 94105; or call 800-677-2082.

◆ *Galante's Venture Capital & Private Equity Directory*, which provides comprehensive information on venture capital and buyout firms. Galante's directory has monthly updates providing information about new sources of venture capital as they materialize. Write to: Asset Alternatives, Inc., 170 Linden Street, Wellesley, MA 02181; or call 781-431-7353.

◆ If you have received at least one round of outside financing, visit **www.ventureone.com** to become part of VentureOne's company database. By doing so, you will put your company in front of the top-tier venture funds that mine this database for investment opportunities. It is free to entrepreneurs.

Pulling Your Research Together

ACCORDING TO TANKERSLEY, IF YOUR RESEARCH INTO VEN-
ture capital firms is done correctly, the process of natural selection will whittle down your list of candidates to a manageable number, somewhere between 10 and 50.

Since directories often contain flaws inherent in the data-gathering process, it's wise to call the venture capital firms you've isolated and ask for brochures, which allow you to see the types of companies in which the firms invest.

Finally, to isolate the top candidates from your research, Tankersley recommends scoring them on a matrix by your search criteria—namely, preferences for leadership, stage of development, geography, deal size, and industry. As shown in the chart at right, by assigning a score for each preference

Ranking Venture Capital Firms

	FUND A	FUND B	FUND C
STAGE OF DEVELOPMENT	1	2	1
INVESTMENT SIZE	1	1	0
GEOGRAPHY	2	2	1
INDUSTRY	1	2	1
LEADERSHIP	1	2	0
SCORE	6	9	3

(2 = good match, 1 = acceptable match, and 0 = poor match), you can get an overall score for each candidate to determine which ones are best.

Testimony to the importance of selecting carefully researched targets is offered by this comment from Gordon Baty, a partner with Zero Stage Capital, a venture capital fund headquartered in Cambridge, Massachusetts: "Of every 100 plans that we get," he says, "90 are completely irrelevant because they do not match our investment criteria regarding the industry, stage of development, geographic location, or the amount of capital we typically invest." From this misguided bunch, Baty says, "our receptionist can weed out their business plans."

The gravest tactical error an entrepreneur can commit, he adds, is to start cold calling venture capitalists. A more likely path to success is to get a referral from one of the usual suspects: an accountant or attorney, with attorneys being the more likely candidate.

The best introduction for an entrepreneur, says Baty, comes from the chief executive of a company Baty has invested in, or who is recognized as an authority in an industry where the fund is active. "To me, the most credible referrals come from people inside the industry," Baty says.

To find the companies that a targeted venture firm has invested in, refer once again to the firm's brochure. The document, says Baty, "should provide you with an embarrassment of riches," including the names of the firm's partners and the firm's area of focus, as well as its auditors, accountants, limited partners, and advisory boards—all of which helps to avoid the pitfalls of cold calling.

If you have truly targeted well, you will know many of the companies on this list. If you are not direct competitors, you can call the chief executives of the companies and ask them about their experiences with the venture capitalist. If the conversation goes well, one may agree to introduce you to their venture capitalist.

In some ways, hunting for venture capital is like painting a room. All the prep work gets done up front; when it's done right, the actual painting is easy. In the same vein, if the preparation of venture capital candidates has been done correctly, the actual calling is easy.

The principles of approaching a venture capitalist and an angel are exactly the same. The only difference is that angels do not have to invest and tend to be cagey about giving a straight yes or no answer. Venture capitalists, on the other hand, are most often fiduciaries, and therefore *must* invest the funds under their control. As a result, if well targeted, they are more likely to read a business plan, make a rapid decision whether or not they are interested, and quickly issue a yes or no answer. As the introduction to this chapter suggests, however, entrepreneurs looking for venture capital must be ready to hear no many more times than yes.

CHAPTER 6

Creative Financing Sources

HE FINANCING SOURCES AND TECHNIQUES
discussed in Chapters 2 through 5 are the most
popular and conventional ones for raising capital.
Still, there are other ways to raise money. The
techniques described below represent some creative
strategies used by entrepreneurs to fund their
businesses. Some are appropriate for companies
that can support a loan, but for one reason or
another cannot get a bank or other lending
institution to back them. Others, however, can be
used by what professional investors often call "raw"
start-ups.

Contact a Community Loan Development Fund

THESE ARE NOT-FOR-PROFIT GROUPS STAFFED BY
community and business leaders, sponsored by
churches, private citizens, and, in some cases,

banks. They make small, community-based loans. These funds aim to improve the quality of life in an area by attracting jobs, and to do this they go where a bank wouldn't dare.

Consider the case of Mike Bryan and Dave Miller, veteran managers of sawmills who longed for a business of their own. When the opportunity came up to buy a closed-down mill for cheap, the pair jumped at the chance. The only problem was capital. They needed about $100,000.

The deal was risky. Not only was the business they had in mind a pure start-up, but mills were closing by the score throughout the Northwest. Not a single bank would touch the deal. However, the Cascadia Revolving Loan Fund, a community loan development group in Seattle, decided to jump in.

According to loan officer Josh Drake, Cascadia stepped forward in December 1995 with $75,000 in equity and a $25,000, five-year term loan. The fund, as well as the surrounding community, has been well rewarded for their confidence in the pair of rough-hewn entrepreneurs. Bryan and Miller's North Star Lumber Company in Shelton, Washington, about 150 miles southwest of Seattle, was profitable in 1996 with $5 million in revenues, and the payroll has grown to 50 employees.

Cascadia's Drake says equity investment, though unusual for a community loan development fund, is a growing trend. To locate a fund near you, call the National Community Capital Association at 215-923-4754.

Put Your Business in an Incubator

INCUBATORS OFFER THEIR SMALL-BUSINESS CLIENTS FINANCIAL and professional assistance that typically includes flexible space and leases, orchestrated exposure to a network of business and technical consultants, access to university resources, and entrée to new business opportunities through cooperative ventures with other incubator clients. According to Dinah Adkins at the National Business Incubation Association in Athens, Ohio, most of the 550 incubators in North America offer some formal or informal access to financing in the form of affiliated angel networks, in-house seed funds, or dedicated revolving loan funds.

Consider the case of Katherine Hammer, founder and chief executive officer of Evolutionary Technologies International, Inc., in Austin, Texas. A former assistant professor of linguistics, Hammer traded in the challenges of ancient Norse dialects in 1991 for the contemporary brainteasers associated with COBOL. She founded Evolutionary Technologies to help large companies with data integration management, and to keep related data on different systems consistent.

After doing basic research at Micro Electronics and Computer Technology Corp. in Austin, Hammer moved across town to the Austin Technology Incubator. According to Hammer, the founder of the incubator was George Kozmatsky, who was also the founder of technology giant Teledyne.

"George provided us with unbelievably helpful counsel and guidance," recalls Hammer.

He also provided her with introductions to an informal network of angels who were affiliated with the incubator. One of these investors, retired admiral Bobby Inman, made a $250,000 commitment that anchored another $1.25 million from other area investors, for a total first-round financing of $1.5 million. "Our acceptance in the incubator carried weight," she says. "By being accepted there, it offered due diligence value to investors." Hammer worked miracles with the capital, and today her Evolutionary Technologies—some say the poster child of the Austin incubator—is profitable with approximately $22 million in sales.

Incubators serve all kinds of businesses. According to Adkins, of the current incubators in operation, 40 percent concentrate on service, 23 percent on light manufacturing, 22 percent on technology, and 7 percent on basic research, with the remaining 8 percent supporting diverse businesses and industries.

To find an incubator near you, send a self-addressed, stamped envelope to: National Business Incubation Association, 20 East Circle Drive, Suite 190, Athens, OH 45701; 614-593-4331.

Utilize Royalty Financing

CONVENTIONAL WISDOM SUGGESTS THAT COMPANIES SELL equity to raise money. However, some try a more creative approach: They sell a piece of their own revenue stream, instead. So-called royalty financing works well in several situations and delivers a host of benefits to early-stage companies.

The technique was used by Terralink Software Systems of South Portland, Maine, to turbocharge its sales and marketing efforts. Terralink developed and sells a PC-based software product to help companies manage hazardous waste information and comply with environmental laws.

Though company founder David Fernald was pleased with the company's growth in sales, he says, "My feeling was we needed to get to $750,000 in sales before repeat and referral business would really kick in, and to get to that level we would need funds to expand our marketing efforts."

However, Fernald faced the typical dilemma of early-stage companies. With Terralink still in its formative stages, investors—whether venture capitalists or angels—would want a big piece of the company. To avoid this dilemma, Fernald turned to royalty financing. Instead of buying straight equity in Terralink, investors put up an advance of $200,000 against future sales. In Terralink's case, the investors were two state economic development organizations.

In exchange for this advance, the investors each received 3 percent of Terralink's sales for 10 years, or until they received payments totaling $600,000. This amount would represent the original $200,000 investment, plus $400,000 more. If Terralink repays the advance over 10 years, investors will earn a compound annual return of 11.6 percent on their investment. If, however, Terralink's sales take off and $600,000 is paid to the investors in five years, their compound annual return will mushroom to 24.5 percent.

Fernald says the technique has several advantages:

◆ First, royalty financings can be easily structured with individual investors. He speculates that a monthly or quarterly return—which happens as long as sales occur—would be more preferable to individual investors than the total absence of a yield and zero liquidity that is typical of early-stage venture deals.

◆ Second, because the royalty advance is, at the end of the day, a loan, it does not invoke any federal or state securities laws that may require complex filings and significant legal fees.

◆ Third, investors taste the fruits of success early and for a prolonged period of time, rather than waiting for the discrete and sometimes elusive payday of an initial public offering (IPO) or a buyout.

◆ Fourth, a company funded by royalty payments becomes more attractive to financiers down the road. Sometimes the presence of one kind of equity investor precludes the participation of other kinds. For instance, a company financed with venture capital cannot, in most cases, ever go back to raising money privately from individuals. However, by "saving" itself for outside investors to a later round of financing, a company keeps its options wide open.

♦ Fifth, and most important, *the royalty structure preserves the equity positions of the founders.*

Fernald says that while royalty financing is a great technique, it's not for everyone. For instance, he says, "It's not a good idea for companies that have very thin margins." After all, if your gross margin (sales less cost of goods sold) is just 10 percent, and 6 percent goes to royalty payments, then the remaining 4 percent doesn't leave much room for making any money. Terralink, for instance, has a gross margin of 90 percent.

Fernald adds that royalty financings work best for companies whose pricing is fairly elastic. "If you can raise your prices to cover the lost margin and not lose customers, you are a better candidate than a company where customers are price sensitive," he says.

In addition, Fernald suggests that royalty financing won't work for companies that do not see an immediate cause and effect between marketing efforts and sales. "You've got to be able to turn on sales like a spigot," he says. Otherwise, one of the primary benefits for which investors are in the deal—namely a monthly royalty check—becomes seriously compromised.

In theory, royalty financing will work for a company that is about to launch a product but doesn't yet have revenues. Obviously, you have to inspire confidence among investors that you have the skills and experience to move products or services off the shelf frequently and quickly.

Finally, royalty financing probably won't solve all of a company's financing needs for all time. But it can definitely deliver a company from the dilemma of giving up too much equity too early on.

For a primer on royalty financing, send a self-addressed stamped envelope to: Banking Dynamics, 97 A Exchange Street, Portland, ME 04101.

If you are located in the northeastern United States, maintain high gross margins, and want to raise $500,000 or less in royalty financing, contact: Royalty Capital Fund, 5 Downing Road, Lexington, MA, 02173; 781-861-8490 (contact: Arthur Fox).

Look Overseas

BELIEVE IT OR NOT, IT'S DIFFERENT HERE. WHILE IN AMERICA it seems that everyone and his brother has a business plan and a deal, there simply isn't the same volume of investment opportunities in Europe, South America, or Asia. Foreign investors have to hunt farther afield to find exciting, young companies with new technologies or new products that can open up vast new markets virtually overnight.

However, there's another factor that can bring foreign investors to your door: licensing and joint-venture opportunities. Many foreign investors want the opportunity to capitalize on new technology, new products, and new business concepts in their immediate geography. They can do that through an investment in a U.S. company, taking licensing rights in their territory as part of the deal.

Consider Larry Fondren, founder, president, and chief executive officer of InterVest of Berwyn, Pennsylvania, a technology company seeking to revolutionize the trading of debt instruments.

The trading market for most corporate and municipal bonds has not kept pace with the technological developments that have driven equity trading. "Rather than the leading-edge technology, bonds rely on the simple technology of phones and faxes," says Fondren. In fact, he says, for most bonds there is very little centralized trading information that lets investors understand trading history, recent prices, and bids from other buyers—all of which is standard for even the humblest of equities that trade on the lowest rung of the Nasdaq stock market, the Bulletin Board.

As a result, the bond market can be terribly inefficient, with hidden costs that have a serious negative impact on the profits of bond investors. Enter Fondren's InterVest, which has developed an electronic market for fixed-income securities (i.e., bonds) through which institutional investors can trade directly with each other without third-party intermediation. The official launch of the system occurred during the first quarter of 1997.

Of course, an idea like this takes capital and plenty of it. After plowing in all he had, plus another $1.5 million borrowed from friends, family, and credit cards, Fondren went looking for more capital. Working with Shamrock Partners, an investment banking firm with offices in New York, Chicago, and Philadelphia, Fondren quickly closed a deal with his first outside investor, Dawnay, Day, a British merchant banking and trading firm. Though merchant bankers are always looking for investments, the InterVest deal demonstrates the synergies that can occur between U.S. firms and their counterparts overseas.

Dawnay, Day, which trades government bonds throughout Europe, invested "not only to get a return, but also to have the ability to license and import technology that would give them a competitive edge in their marketplace," according to Fondren. Indeed, the InterVest technology was just the kind of system that Dawnay, Day would soon find itself competing against, and to have it in their arsenal was a powerful strategic advantage.

Naturally, Fondren wanted capital, but he also wanted something more. "Our business has global potential," he says. "But trading bonds in the United States is tricky enough. To take our system, say, into Europe, we needed a local partner that knew the subtleties, conventions, and regulations in the many different markets there."

According to Shamrock's Joseph Huard, the United Kingdom, Germany, and the advanced economies of the Pacific Rim, such as Japan and Malaysia, are where interest in American companies is highest. "These countries have many large businesses that are well established and forward looking," says Huard. "But they do not necessarily have the infrastructure to support growing companies that are so commonplace here."

Moreover, Huard adds that in many of these countries, consensus and the status quo rule, not the engineer in the laboratory with unconventional ideas that lead to new products and services. Accordingly, he says, there's not likely to be a surge in entrepreneurialism anytime soon that will detract from the interest in American companies.

Key requirements for success in raising capital overseas, says Huard, are products or services that are universal in appeal but for which, at least initially, there is a specific target or clientele. Unfortunately, unless you have relatives overseas, finding investors there is probably too risky to attempt without professional guidance. "It's still a wild world out there," says Fondren. "Without a professional who knows the territory, you could find yourself quickly lost and in trouble."

Get a Margin Loan from a Wealthy Investor

WEALTHY INDIVIDUALS WHO TYPICALLY DO NOT INVEST IN emerging companies might be convinced to do so utilizing margin loans, according to Steve Cohen, once a financing consultant who helped raise capital for emerging companies and now a vice president of finance for Tradepoint of America, in New York City.

Here's how it works: Individuals with large investments in the stock market take a loan out against their holdings in a particular security. For instance, if an investor owns $200,000 of Consolidated Edison, the brokerage firm holding the stock will loan the investor $100,000 or more. This is called a margin loan, and margin interest rates, because the loan is fully collateralized, are typically from one to one-and-a-half points below prime.

The investor then lends the proceeds of the margin loan to the entrepreneur, utilizing a promissory note. The terms of the note are simple, says Cohen. "The borrower agrees to pay the margin interest plus a premium of perhaps 3 percent, plus any margin calls." A margin call occurs when the value of the stock collateralizing the loan falls below the value of the loan. This happens when the price of the stock declines, and brokerage firms call their customers and ask them to make up the difference.

Cohen says that stock market investors will often make

this kind of deal because it doesn't cost them anything, leaves all of their personal capital at their disposal, and if all goes well, lets them enjoy a certain amount of leverage from their stock market holdings. The very real risk to entrepreneurs, says Cohen, is that they may have to make what amounts to principal payments on funds they did not borrow when their lender gets a margin call. Naturally, this source of capital is more appropriate for companies that can support a principal and interest payment but which, for one reason or another, can't get the commitment of a bank.

Venture Capital, Federal Government Style

THE FEDERAL GOVERNMENT'S STAB AT VENTURE CAPITAL BEGAN in 1958 when Congress launched the Small Business Investment Company (SBIC) program. The feds quite correctly reasoned that there were few places indeed where an entrepreneur could turn for the kind of patient, private equity capital that a business would need to get launched.

SBICs are private investment firms or partnerships that are licensed by the Small Business Administration (SBA). These private investment companies have their own minimum capital of $5 million, and through an SBA license, are able to obtain access to government-guaranteed debentures and other debt financing. By doing so, an SBIC can leverage its capital position and therefore do more deals. An SBIC can leverage its capital by as much as 300 percent. Thus, an SBIC with $10 million in private capital can borrow another $30 million at favorable rates with an SBA guarantee.

SBICs are for businesses that can support a loan with regular payments but, for one reason or another, are not bankable. A typical SBIC deal will involve subordinated debt—debt that gets paid off after so-called senior debt in the event of liquidation—with some sort of equity kicker. The equity kicker usually takes the form of warrants or options that grant the SBIC the right to buy stock at favorable prices if the company prospers. The important point to remember is that although SBICs will generally take more risk than a banker, the underlying instrument of financing is debt, which requires a regular stream of payments.

As a case in point, consider Indianapolis-based Micro-Link Corporation. The company, which developed Standard computer boards, saw plenty of opportunity in the $1.5 billion market for VME computer boards. The designation VME stands for Virtual Modular Eurocard and refers to size and design specifications that make the boards appropriate for harsh operating environments such as factories, military outposts, and highway monitoring stations. To develop a line of VME cards, Micro-Link needed financing, according to Chief Financial Officer Larry Morton.

Though the company had an established history of sales and earnings from its Standard computer boards, the deal wasn't bankable per se because the proceeds were for product development, around which there was too much uncertainty regarding the ability to create new products and the market's response to these products if successfully developed. However, for a local SBIC, the deal, though risky, was more appealing. As a result, Micro-Link received $525,000 in financing and was able to successfully develop a full line of VME products that now constitute a staple of its product offerings.

Virtually identical to SBICs are Specialized Small Business Investment Companies, or SSBICs. The primary difference is that SSBICs offer financing to businesses owned by socially or economically disadvantaged persons.

One of the largest SSBICs, Freshstart Venture Capital Corp. of New York City, focuses on financing taxicab medallions, which account for 70 percent of its loan portfolio. These deals represent a viable market for Freshstart because many taxis are owned by immigrants; because the taxis are on the crowded New York City streets for as much as 16 hours a day, there's plenty of cash flow.

There are approximately 220 SBICs and 80 SSBICs. To find one near you, contact the National Association of Small Business Investment Companies, 666 11th Street NW, Suite 750, Washington, DC 20001; 202-628-5055. This association represents primarily SBICs, but its membership list, which is made available upon request, includes member SSBICs as well. Also contact the National Association of Investment Companies, which is the trade association of SSBICs, at 111 14th Street NW, Suite 700, Washington, DC 20005; 202-289-4336.

State and Federal Government Assistance

THE STATES AND THE FEDERAL GOVERNMENT HAVE FOUND A positive correlation between their investments in technology/agriculture and job creation/tax revenues. For instance, Pennsylvania's cumulative investment in technology between 1983 and 1994 of $265 million generated more than $640 million in matching private-sector funds and more than $88 million in federal funds. For Pennsylvania, the bottom-line results have been equally impressive: 16,000-plus new jobs, 1,000 expansions by existing corporations, 824 new businesses, and more than 700 new products and manufacturing processes.

With results like these, it should come as no surprise that the states and the federal government have a myriad of technology cooperative programs that can provide funding for capital-hungry entrepreneurs.

At the state level, it's important to keep in mind that not all programs provide access to capital. Many programs are about assistance. Other programs offer assistance as their mainstay but have some kind of funding buried deep within. For instance, in Florida, the publicly and privately supported nonprofit group Enterprise Florida oversees three programs through its affiliate, Innovation Partnership. These three are the Innovation Commercialization Corporations (ICCs), the Technology Research Investment Fund (TRIF), and the Florida Manufacturing Technology Center (FMTC). The ICCs aid and abet technology transfer while the FMTC helps manufacturers resolve technical problems. However, the TRIF will "show you the money." In 1994 it financed 37 companies to the tune of $30,000 to $50,000 each for product development efforts. In almost all 50 states, similar scenarios are likely to be found.

At the federal level, things really got going in 1980. Faced with industrial competitiveness issues, the feds started pouring resources into technology transfer with landmark legislation, such as the Stevenson-Wydler Technology Innovation Act of 1980, the Small Business Innovation Development Act of 1982, and the Defense Conversion Reinvestment and Transition Assistance Act of 1992.

Like state efforts, many of these acts have resulted in assistance programs to aid the transfer and commercialization of technology or industrial problem solving. However, many others are about finance. For instance, the Small Business Innovation Research (SBIR) program, which came into being with the Small Business Innovation Development Act of 1982, mandates that agencies with annual research budgets of more than $100 million provide research grants and contracts to small businesses, ranging from $55,000 to $750,000. Today, 11 federal government departments, agencies, and administrations participate in the SBIR program, with aggregate grants approaching $1 billion.

Getting funding from the government, state or federal, is about as difficult as getting money from equity investors, but for different reasons. First, governments by nature are difficult to deal with and can daunt even the most enthusiastic entrepreneurs with red tape. Second, governments are so large, it's sometimes difficult to know exactly where the money is. I can't do anything about the first problem. The second problem, however, has a solution. Purchase the book *Partnerships,* by Dan Berglund and Christopher Coburn (with a foreword by Al Gore). This impressive tome lists each state's programs, as well as federal programs, by agency with phone numbers, addresses, and contact information. This is a must for anyone who wants to ask what their government can do for them. (*Partnerships: A Compendium of State and Federal Cooperative Technology Programs,* Battelle Press, 505 King Avenue, Columbus, OH 43201; 800-451-3543; **www.battelle.org/bookstore**.)

Tap Your 401(k)

FOR WOULD-BE ENTREPRENEURS CUT LOOSE FROM CORPORATE America with a 401(k) plan, capital is right at their fingertips. They need only set up an employee stock-ownership plan (ESOP) in their new company and have their 401(k) purchase shares from the ESOP.

In truth, it's a tricky transaction, but the benefits are compelling: Capital can be raised without the time or expense of seeking outside investors, and most important, founders do not give up any equity. In addition, if the company grows and employees participate in the plan, founding shareholders get a built-in exit strategy, since the ESOP will purchase their shares at fair market value.

"Every accountant, attorney, and securities professional I spoke with told me the transaction could not be done because 401(k) plans are prohibited from investing in private companies," says Jim O'Brien, one of the founders of Print Management Partners, based in Des Plaines, Illinois. Attorney Greg Brown, however, an ESOP specialist with Seyfarth, Shaw, Fairweather & Geraldson of Chicago, said with little fanfare but a great deal of confidence that such a transaction *could* be done and went on to engineer one for Print Management Partners.

Brown, who is the head of the Legislative and Regulatory Advisory Committee for the ESOP Association, Washington, D.C., says that many professionals don't think 401(k) financing is viable for small, private companies because they believe the issuance of stock to employees requires a full-blown registration statement, similar to registrations filed when a company goes public. "If that were the case," says Brown, "this technique probably wouldn't work for small companies." However, he says, companies can issue stock under Rule 701 of the Securities Act of 1933 for compensatory benefit programs. "Benefit-plan registrations," says Brown, "are much easier to complete, and much less expensive to file, which makes them viable for emerging companies."

Print Management Partners was formed when six associates from a large label and forms printer left en masse, each taking with them a 401(k). Working with Brown, a valuation specialist, an accountant, and a brokerage firm to act as custodian, the principals of the new firm were able to tap their 401(k)s to the tune of $427,000 for equipment, receivables, and inventory. There were no adverse tax consequences, and the company did not relinquish any equity to outsiders. While their 401(k)s still hold other securities, Jim O'Brien, one of Print Management's founders, feels confident about the investment in his own company. "This was the safest investment we could make because we understand the business inside and out and have control over its destiny."

Securing
Investor
Support

SECT

CHAPTER 7

Valuing Your Business

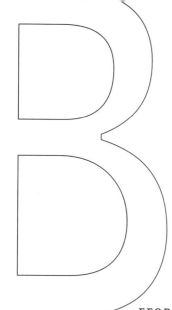

EFORE ANY OF THE EQUITY INVESTORS mentioned in the preceding chapters can become *your* investors, you must cross one great divide: the price. While the entrepreneur and the investor may agree that the business requires $1 million to jump-start production and marketing, there is likely to be little agreement on just what percentage of ownership the investor will get for providing this amount of capital. Ultimately, for the two to get a deal done, there must be agreement on the *value* of the enterprise. This single number is the anvil upon which the rest of the deal will be hammered out because it defines the ownership positions of investor and entrepreneur.

While equity investors have differing profiles and entrepreneurs certainly come in every stripe, the dance around valuation is always the same. On one side of the table, the entrepreneur is trying to protect his or her precious percentage points of equity. There are only 100 percentage points to start with, and over several rounds of financing they disappear with alarming ease. For instance, modern Internet legends David Filo and Jerry Yang, who founded Yahoo!, had sold 70 percent of their company to venture capitalists and public investors by the time their April 1996 initial public offering (IPO) was complete.

On the other side of the table, equity investors are trying not to overpay. A business might be worth $5 million. However, if a case can be made for a valuation of $3 million, the $1 million the investor is prepared to sink into the company can be a 33 percent ownership, versus 20 percent of a $5 million-dollar business. Simply by arguing persuasively, equity investors can increase their ownership position by more than 50 percent.

Entrepreneurs always tend to think their businesses are worth more than do investors. Except for really stellar companies, however, investors tend to win the battle on valuation. Why? Because investors own the gold. In early-stage finance, as in many other walks in life, he or she who owns the gold makes the rules.

This chapter is about valuing your company in the same way an equity investor does. In addition, it provides you with the tools you need to make the case for a premium valuation.

Why You Must Value Your Business before Talking with Investors

"IT'S ABSOLUTELY AMAZING," REMARKS JOHN LANE, AN investment banker in Westport, Connecticut, who specializes in emerging growth companies, "how many companies looking for capital have not done any fundamental analysis to determine what their business is worth, or are shopping deals with utterly ridiculous valuations."

You separate your deal from the pack with a well-conceived valuation analysis. It is important to have a clearly defined and well-delineated argument for your company's valuation, says Lane, because, except for those who specialize in one industry, "most equity investors have little concept of what a company is worth and need some guidance." The situation is analogous to consumers making big-ticket purchases. When there's a lot of money at stake, consumers carefully read product marketing literature to understand why the product costs as much as it does. Without this information many will simply move on to another brand.

In the same vein, without a valuation on the table, many equity investors—particularly high-strung and perennially overworked investment bankers—might not take discussions with an entrepreneur to the next step. It's not that they *can't*. There's just a greater likelihood that they *won't*. With raising capital so difficult to begin with, why make the task even harder?

Entrepreneurs who look for equity capital without a valuation also give up the high ground and may surrender more equity than they have to. "The advantage they lose," says Lane, "is that rather than *telling* the investor how much their company is worth and why, the entrepreneur ends up *listening* to the investor's assessment of how little their company is worth and why."

The problem worsens when investors undertake the kind of analytical research that the entrepreneur should have done in the first place. When doing this research, investors often develop a stubborn conviction about the value of the company. Therefore, know ahead of time what your company is worth and why.

A Framework for Measuring Value

WHILE THERE ARE MANY WAYS TO VALUE A BUSINESS, FOR THE purpose of raising capital it makes sense to develop a valuation analysis that answers the question that's on investors' minds. Specifically, what will this company be worth in three or five years? And what is it worth today?

By far, the most widely used technique for doing this is the so-called *discounted cash flow method.* It is the method most professional investors use to assess value, and therefore the one you should have at your disposal to meet an investor on his or her turf.

The discounted cash flow method relies on two concepts that, when initially introduced, often prove slippery to grasp. The first and easier of the two concepts to understand is that the value of an enterprise is some multiple of what it earns. The second concept is that all future cash flows are equal to some present day amount.

Regarding the first concept, for argument's sake assume that by divine intervention it is known that businesses are worth five times their net income. Thus, the business earning $100,000 is worth $500,000, or simply: 5 x $100,000. That's easy to understand. What's far more difficult to assess, however, is just what the multiple ought to be, a topic that is covered later on.

Parenthetically, it's worth noting that the concept of a multiple probably has its roots in the bond market. After all, a bond paying 7.5 percent, or $75 per year, costs the investor $1,000. The $1,000 bond is valued at 13.3 times the $75 cash flow it generates. Logic would dictate that if the bond were a higher risk, the payment would be higher and the multiple would be lower. If the bond had little risk, the payment would be lower and the multiple higher. *Hmmm.*

The second concept related to value says that an investor whose required rate of return is 5 percent has no preference between receiving $1.00 today or receiving $1.05 one year from today. Why? Because if the investor gets $1.00 today, he or she will simply invest it at 5 percent and end up with $1.05 a year from now. Therefore, the *present value* of $1.05 received one year from today, for this investor, is $1.00.

Note that the investor whose required rate of return is 25 percent has a different set of numbers to work with. This investor is indifferent between $1.00 today and $1.25 a year from now. If the second investor were to receive the first investor's $1.05 a year from now, what would he or she need to receive today in order to hit his or her required rate of return of 25 percent? Eighty-four cents. Said differently, $0.84 invested at 25 percent per year will yield $1.05 a year from now, making the second investor indifferent between the two sums.

Applying this concept to a business suggests its future income can also be reduced to a present value. Thus, the $1 million (before taxes) a business is expected to earn three years from now is equal to $657,000 today for the investor whose required rate of return is 15 percent ($1 million / 1.15^3). Now add in the concept of a multiple. If the multiple remains at the above-decreed five times earnings, the business earning $1 million in three years could arguably be worth $5 million at that time ($1 million x 5). The present value of this future value would be about $3.3 million ($5 million / 1.15^3). If the owner of this hypothetical business were looking for $1 million in equity capital, he or she might consider giving up about 30 percent of the business ($1 million / $3.3 million) to the investor.

Measuring Value: A Case in Point

HOW DOES ALL THIS WORK WITH A REAL COMPANY? CONSIDER the experience of Philadelphia-based entrepreneur Rod Vahle, who has been in the pet-supply business for 30 years. As of 1996, he had nine pet-supply and animal-theme gift stores, called Accent on Animals, up and running. Originally, Vahle's shops offered supplies only. But by adding pet-related items such as cards, clothing, stationery, and books alongside traditional supplies, Vahle found that he could generate substantially higher margins than pet super-stores or traditional gift shops.

Vahle put together a business plan to roll out 250 more stores and estimated he needed initial capital of $6 million to do it. For Vahle, equity capital was the only way to go. He had spent 30 years building a nine-store chain using debt. However, with a nice, patient $6 million dollop of equity, Vahle felt he could make a quantum leap in his rollout rate.

His first big question was, "What is my business worth and how much equity will I have to give up for the $6 million that I need?" To answer this, Vahle had to estimate his future earnings, calculate their present value, and determine the appropriate multiple for these earnings.

As for estimating earnings, Vahle had to decide which of his five years of future operating earnings should be used. Although five-year projections are standard, the fifth-year estimates are too unreliable to be used for estimating the value of the business. In truth, most investors ask for five-year projections because they want to see, on an order-of-magnitude basis, just how large the entrepreneur wants the business to become.

For the purpose of estimating value, use third-year projected operating earnings. It is close enough so that investors can envision the time period in the context of what entrepreneurs say they will accomplish, but far enough away so that significant earnings, hence value, can be created. In Vahle's case, the projected operating earnings in the third year were $3 million. (Although this did not apply to Vahle, if projected operating earnings have significant noncash charges, such as depreciation, you should use annual cash flow instead.)

Next, Vahle had to decide which discount rate to use. This number is critical to the mathematical equation used to determine the present value of future earnings:

$$\text{Present Value} = \text{Future Earnings, Year 3} / (1 + \text{Discount Rate})^3$$

Notice that the smaller the denominator, the larger the present value. The larger the denominator, the smaller the present value. Translation: *The present value of a company is inversely related to the discount rate.* That is, the larger the discount rate used in the equation, the smaller the present value of the company. The smaller the discount used, the larger the present value of the company.

Intuitively then, the business owner would use the lowest possible discount rate, say 5 percent, to calculate the present value of future earnings. If Vahle did this, he would arrive at a present value of $2.6 million for his future earnings of $3 million ($3 million / 1.05³). Obviously, this is a much better figure than the $1.2 million that he would get using a discount rate of 35 percent ($3 million / 1.35³). But is 5 percent realistic?

No, because the discount rate is the investor's required rate of return, and no investor investing in early-stage enterprises will settle for a return of 5 percent per year. To see why the discount rate is the investor's required rate of return, consider the following rearrangement of the above present-value formula. It goes like this:

$$\text{Future Earnings, Year 3} = \text{Present Earnings} (1 + \text{Discount Rate})^3$$

Thus, the discount rate is the factor by which present earnings are advanced so that they reach the desired future value. So, what's the appropriate discount rate? *Twenty-five percent.*

This figure owes its origin to venture capital funds, which strive to achieve a compound annual rate of return of 25 percent on successful investments. Even if you are negotiating with angels, they will understand the risks they are taking and will demand a return comparable to those earned by venture capital investors.

The 25 percent figure is also benchmarked with ongoing research by Satya Pradhuman, manager of U.S. quantitative analysis for Merrill Lynch in New York City. According to Pradhuman, over the past 20 years so-called microcapitalization companies (public companies whose stock price times total shares outstanding are valued at $100 million or less) outperformed the market at large with a compound annual rate of return of 19.54 percent. By comparison, over the past 20 years the S&P 500 returned 15.51 percent. Therefore, the argument goes, if high-risk public companies return almost 20 percent, high-risk companies that are not yet public must offer investors a premium, ergo, 25 percent.

Using this discount rate, the $3 million that Vahle's Accent on Animals will earn in the third year after funding has a present value of $1.53 million to the investor willing to take on the kind of risk that Vahle's venture entails.

Now that Vahle knows that the present value of his earnings is $1.53 million, he needs an earnings multiple to calculate a valuation for his business that he can present to investors. The task of finding an appropriate earnings multiple can be accomplished quite easily by looking at the price/earnings (P/E) ratios enjoyed by similar public companies.

What do the P/E ratios mean? In essence, they are formulas for measuring the value of the price of a share of stock. A common stock that is trading at $15 per share and that has earnings per share of $2, would have a P/E ratio of 7.5 ($15 / $2). In other words, the common stock is valued at seven-and-a-half times its earnings. However, since a share of stock is just a microcosm of the company, the same formula can be used to value the enterprise at large. Thus, Vahle's Accent on Animals can also be valued at 7.5 times earnings, less any debt he might have on the books.

However, is 7.5 the right factor? Should it be higher? Or should it be lower? To answer these questions, Vahle needs to look at public companies like his own and find their multiples. After all, the price of publicly held common stock represents the consensus of informed buyers and sellers. Therefore, the multiple at which a particular group of companies trades represents a tenable measure of value.

In general, industry groups have different multiples, depending on the overall prospects for the segment. For instance, here are some multiples from Standard & Poor's *Analysts' Handbook*.

Price/Earnings Ratios by Industry

SECTOR	P/E RATIO
COMPOSITE INDEX	19.7
AUTO PARTS & EQUIPMENT	10.6
BANKS	13.9
COMPUTER HARDWARE	31.4
COMPUTER SOFTWARE	50.4
DIVERSIFIED CHEMICALS	15.7
ELECTRONICS (INSTRUMENTATION)	31.3
INVESTMENT BANKING/BROKERAGE	8.8
MANUFACTURING, DIVERSIFIED	18.4
MEDICAL PRODUCTS, SUPPLIES	29.2
METALS MINING	14.4
PHOTOGRAPHY, IMAGING	23.9
PUBLISHING, NEWSPAPERS	38.4
RESTAURANTS	22.0
RETAIL (DEPARTMENT STORES)	18.2
SERVICES (ADVERTISING/MARKETING)	24.7
TELEPHONE	14.7
TOBACCO	12.8
TRUCKS & PARTS	11.1
WASTE MANAGEMENT	15.9

Note the wide variations. Investors are buying software companies high and banks low. Said differently, investors were willing to fork over, on average, 50.4 times what a share of stock earns in order to be invested in software, but only 13.9 times earnings for banking companies. Individual equities bear this out. As 1997 came to a close, Microsoft (Nasdaq: MSFT) was trading at 53 times earnings, and Citicorp New York Stock Exchange (NYSE: CCI) was trading at 17 times earnings.

Instead of the P/E ratio, a company can also use its projected growth rate as a valuation multiple. The higher of the two should be used because investors who want to haggle over valuation will employ the lower. In practice, this means that if a company earns $10 million and enjoys a compound annual growth in earnings of 20 percent, the business at large can be valued at $200 million ($10 million x 20), less any debt it has outstanding. With 10 million shares issued and outstanding, each one should be trading at $20 per share ($200 million / 10 million shares). If this particular equity were trading at, say, $18, security analysts might suggest that the company was undervalued because it was trading at a discount to its growth rate.

Vahle, however, chooses to use comparable P/E multiples. The average P/E multiple for Standard & Poor's category of general merchandise retailers is 23.5. This offers a good starting point; however, Vahle will have to dig deeper.

Happily, there are two publicly traded pet-supply stores that represent excellent comparables. There's Petco, which operates 275 pet-food-and-supply stores in 14 states and trades on the Nasdaq National Market System (NMS) under the symbol PETC. And there is (presumably arch rival) PETs-MART (Nasdaq NMS: PETM), based in Phoenix, Arizona, operating some 280 pet-supply superstores in 32 states.

Three "comps," or comparable P/E multiples, are pretty good, but Vahle might need a little more ammunition to make his case. Frequently entrepreneurs can make their arguments with companies that are similarly structured but perhaps in a slightly different line of business. For instance, Natural Wonders (Nasdaq NMS: NATW) of Fremont, California, operates a 146-store chain that sells nature and science products. Like Accent on Animals, Natural Wonders stores are smaller and sell to consumers with an interest in nature; and with 146 locations, the company is almost exactly the size of the empire Vahle is trying to build—at least initially.

There is also Dollar General (NYSE: DG) of Nashville, Tennessee, which owns and operates more than 2,500 general merchandise stores in midwestern and southeastern states. Like Accent on Animals, Dollar General is offering merchandise typically at $1, $5, and $10 price points.

Still another comp might be Dollar Tree Stores (Nasdaq: DLTR) of Norfolk, Virginia, which operates 686 discount variety stores. Like Accent on Animals, Dollar Tree is concentrating on low price points. In addition, Dollar Tree, like Vahle's shops, operates primarily out of strip shopping centers. The chart below shows these comparisons in spreadsheet format.

What are the numbers saying? That investors are paying for growth. The companies that delivered the highest growth in earnings—Petco, Dollar Tree Stores, and PETsMART—were afforded the highest multiples, 40 and beyond. Those companies that delivered slower growth—Dollar General and Natural Wonders—appeared to be somewhat penalized, on a comparative basis. This analysis also shows just how ruthless the consensus opinion of investors can be. Even though Dollar General's earnings performance has achieved a remarkable 35 percent compound annual growth, investors apparently aren't letting the company rest on past laurels.

Vahle now needs to use this information, plus more he has unearthed about the financial performance of his comparables, to suggest why his company should be valued the same as, or perhaps even higher than, the comparable companies. Vahle's analysis goes as follows:

Comparable Valuation Analysis

	12-MONTH REVENUES ($ MILLIONS)	12-MONTH EARNINGS PER SHARE	3-YEAR COMPOUND REVENUE GROWTH
PETCO	270	0.71	32 PERCENT
PETSMART	1,030	0.22	55 PERCENT
NATURAL WONDERS	138	0.23	5 PERCENT
DOLLAR GENERAL STORES	1,764	1.00	24 PERCENT
DOLLAR TREE STORES	300	0.76	35 PERCENT
S&P GEN'L MERCHANDISE RETAILERS	N/A	N/A	N/A

*DURING THE FOURTH QUARTER OF 1996
**PETSMART ACTUALLY DELIVERED A LOSS FOR THE PERIOD UNDER CONSIDERATION. THE COMPANY'S STRATEGY OF ACQUISITIONS PRODUCED A HIGH VOLUME OF EXTRAORDINARY AND NONRECURRING EXPENSES.

- Accent on Animals' actual gross margins, at 45 percent, beat Petco's gross margin of 24 percent by 21 percentage points, and PETsMART's 25 percent gross margin by 20 percentage points.
- Vahle's capital requirements to open new stores are dramatically lower than Petco's and PETsMART's. For instance, to open one of its superstores, PETsMART will spend between $680,000 and $1.2 million. By contrast, Vahle can open a new site for no more than $120,000. The high capital requirements of opening new stores, which is a function of their gargantuan size, helps explain the lower gross margins at Petco and PETsMART.
- Accent on Animals' sales per square foot, $258, are more than 50 percent higher than Petco's $169, and 61 percent higher than PETsMART's $157.
- Vahle's operating earnings per square foot of $39 are more than 10 times the $3.42 Petco enjoys (before nonrecurring expenses are taken into account).
- Accent on Animals' operating margin of 15 percent is more than 300 percent higher than either of its competitors in the pet-supply industry.

Obviously, Vahle is onto something here. He's got a concept that works, and from a profitability standpoint, outper-

3-YEAR COMPOUND EARNINGS GROWTH	RECENT* PRICE	CAPITALIZATION ($ MILLIONS)	P/E RATIO	PRICE/ SALES	PRICE/ BOOK
156 PERCENT	23.75	388	46	1.4	2.3
N/A**	26.00	2,743	46	2.7	9.4
(32 PERCENT)	5.12	40	22	0.3	0.8
35 PERCENT	28.50	2,467	28	1.4	5.5
45 PERCENT	39.25	1,105	40	2.4	14.1
N/A	N/A	N/A	23.5	N/A	N/A

forms all the rocket science of the big boys. Because of this, he can make the case that Accent on Animals ought to be valued just as richly as Petco and PETsMART. Theoretically, Vahle could argue for a valuation using the average multiple of his comparables:

PV of earnings	x	Multiple	=	Valuation
$1.53 million		23.5		$35.9 million

Or he could make an argument that Accent on Animals should be valued using the top multiple in the industry—that is, the P/E ratio of 46 maintained by Petco and PETsMART:

PV of earnings	x	Multiple	=	Valuation
$1.53 million		46		$70.4 million

Bringing Your Valuation Back to Earth

VAHLE HAS DONE HIS HOMEWORK AND HAS A WELL-HONED argument that will help him in negotiations. However, Jim Twaddell, an investment banker in Providence, Rhode Island with more than 25 years of experience financing emerging companies, says, "These numbers simply represent a starting point. Entrepreneurs must then submit themselves to the reality of the situation and leave lots of the theoretical value they find on the table."

Entrepreneurs go into shock when they see how, in the hands of an angel, this "theoretical value" melts like ice cream on a scorching July day. Here's how an angel putting funds into Accent on Animals in a private transaction might pare down Vahle's numbers from the top industry multiple of 46:

◆ **Risk, deduct 33 percent.** Although Vahle has an admirable track record, his company's future earnings, upon which the entire valuation is built, are simply speculation. There is a strong likelihood that earnings will not occur as anticipated; if they don't, the investor will have overpaid dearly. Therefore, the earnings multiple of 46 is now 30.

◆ **Liquidity, deduct 50 percent.** An investor can trade Petco and PETsMART all day long. However, even if Vahle hits his projections and merits his valuation, the investor still has little more than a perceived paper gain. The earnings multiple of 30 gets adjusted down to 15.

◆ **Market pitch, deduct 33 percent.** Just because the stock market has been on a tear for the past few years doesn't necessarily have an influence on what an angel is willing to pay in a private transaction. After all, the S&P 500 gained 37 percent in 1995 and more than 20 percent in 1996. If the entrepreneur and the investor had met two years earlier, with all other business factors being the same, the earnings multiples prevailing in the market at that time might have been much lower. "So I should overpay because Wall Street wants to have a good year?" the investor begins to wonder. Suddenly, Vahle's earnings multiple of 15 is now 10.

If Vahle presents this argument to the investor, and utilizes an earnings multiple of 10, then Accent on Animals will be valued at about $15 million, which is 10 times $1.53 million, the present value of the company's earnings. Finally, the $6 million equity investment should represent 40 percent of Accent on Animals ($6 million / $15 million).

It is important to point out that without all of the comparative financial information showing how Accent on Animals can be a superior financial performer, the starting point could have been much *lower*. After all, if Accent on Animals can't beat the margins delivered by Petco and PETsMART, why should it be, at least initially, afforded the same multiple?

Investment banker Twaddell says that if Accent on Animals were contemplating an initial public offering (IPO) instead of raising the money privately, the multiple would be much higher, since the liquidity and market-pitch issues would disappear. In fact, frothy markets are precisely why many companies choose to go public even though they don't need the capital. Not only is the market more receptive to IPOs, the companies themselves benefit from the premium valuations that the market has bestowed more or less on a wholesale basis.

So-called market exuberance notwithstanding, Twaddell says, "The firm taking the company public would value Accent on Animals below the market leaders because as a younger, smaller, and untested public company, investors would demand a discount to the company's more seasoned peers." Private companies going public are generally valued at discounts to the market ranging from 10 percent to 30 percent.

If an investment were made at this level, would Vahle be getting whacked too hard on the valuation? Probably not. The fact that he is up and running and can point to performance measures that actually exceed his competitors' makes strong arguments he can use to prevent the valuation from going any lower.

However, one thing is for sure. Doing the investor's homework pays off in a big way. If the investor stuck a valuation of $10 million on the company more or less arbitrarily, Vahle would have to fight uphill to get the other $5 million in value his company is worth. The ultimate cost to him could be 20 percent more of the company than might have been otherwise.

This analysis doesn't provide much help for entrepreneurs who need funding for products or services that are not yet launched or developed. Specifically, how can entrepreneurs make compelling arguments about what their companies are worth without any actual performance figures to point to? The answer is: They can't. As venture capitalist John Martinson of the Edison Fund points out, "Valuations for companies at the pre-revenue stage, in their seed or first-round financing, are almost always less than $2 million. It's hard to make a return if it's any higher."

It's not that the above mathematical arguments don't hold for companies at the pre-revenue stage. They do. At early stages, the required rate of return, hence the discount rate, is so large that the present values get reduced to almost nothing.

Investors might not be quite so numerical in reaching this conclusion. Intuitively, though, they're thinking: "If I'm going to put this much money into the company at this stage of its development, I need to own 60 percent of it, period." By now the trend should be clear. If you've got a dream and a team, in terms of value, you don't have much more than that.

CHAPTER 8

Presenting Financials

INVESTORS FREQUENTLY SAY THEY DON'T PAY much attention to financial projections because such numbers are a stab in the dark. For instance, Ted Schlein, a partner with powerhouse venture capital firm Kleiner, Perkins, Caufield & Byers in Menlo Park, California, says, "We will spend 10 minutes going over the financial projections versus three hours on the strategic issues."

It is hard to argue with the approach taken by Kleiner, Perkins. With deals such as Tandem Computers, Genentech, and Netscape to its credit, Kleiner, Perkins clearly knows its stuff. However, Schlein's comment applies only to financial forecasts that appear *reasonable* to begin with. Projections that are way off the mark won't get even 10 minutes.

Another reason that financial projections must be done carefully is that they are a window on an entrepreneur's thinking. It is through this window that investors frequently peer. Here is what they're looking at: Does the company seem to understand how long it will take to collect receivables? Does the cost of goods sold reflect industry norms? Are the assumptions on the frequency and timing of repeat business reasonable? Is the commitment to R&D realistic? Do the marketing costs reflect an understanding of the distribution channel? And on and on it goes.

Finally, the role of financial projections in valuing a company cannot be underestimated. Investment banker Jim Twaddell reiterates: "The future value of the business is *the* central number upon which the equity investor focuses. And it is the financial projections, to the exclusion of any other number, that show what this future value can be."

Almost as important as projections are the

company's historical financial statements. The ability of entrepreneurs to discuss their financial history also provides a window on their thinking. In addition, historical performance is the most credible evidence business owners have at their disposal to support the contentions of projected financial performance.

Raising money from outside investors is fundamentally an act of financial communication. Ultimately, success is a function of financial-presentation skills. This chapter shows how to develop both historical financial statements and projections that speak to the needs of equity investors. Rather than a line-by-line exercise in developing financial projections, the next sections deal with their conceptual framework. In addition, we'll stick with the income statement only, since the balance sheet and cash-flow statements grow out of it.

How to Develop Financial Projections for Equity Investors

ENTREPRENEURS MUST WORK THROUGH EACH LINE OF THE income statement and present a credible picture of the company's future performance. Each line, of course, must be consistent in the context of all of the others.

◆ **Estimating sales.** Given all of the importance laid upon earnings, it's amazing how much attention is paid to revenue. After all, a company with $100 million in revenues and $101 million in expenses doesn't have an ounce of value. Still, revenue is the starting point from which everything flows, so it's got to be right.

Established companies have it all over upstarts because they have some historically proven algorithm to predict future sales. Even if they've never thought about it, it's there. For instance, historically:

1 Each salesperson generated 15 sales per month.
2 Response rate on direct mail was 1.1 percent, for which the subsequent pay-up rate was 92 percent.
3 Each new manufacturer's representative generated $750,000 in sales.

4 Each 30-minute infomercial generated 7,000 inquiries and 400 sales.
5 Sales representatives closed on 12 percent of appointments.
6 Sales/media buy ratio was 1.25.
7 Revenue per tabletop was $12,000.
8 Cash flow from each well, net after drilling costs, was $350,000.

If it's historical and well documented, it's credible. However, where entrepreneurs go wrong in projected revenues is in suggesting a future performance that deviates significantly from the past record, a malaise that undermines the presentation. If your projected revenues are going to depart substantially from past experience, there needs to be a good reason why. Without a good reason, the projections are not credible.

For example, Dermaceutical Labs, Inc. (DLI) of Idaho Falls, Idaho, was selling a line of skin-care products through direct-response television commercials. Historically, the company's sales were 1.25 times its expenditures on media—a lot, but within industry norms. The name of the game was media buying. The more commercials the company could run, the more sales it could make. However, DLI's projections made the assumption that the ratio going forward would be 1.50. Why? According to DLI founder and president Marvin Taylor, "Once the company was funded, we would develop a new series of infomercials with better production values that would feature a celebrity spokesperson. We were confident that with these improvements, our TV infomercials would pull much better." Fair enough. At least 83 percent of Taylor's assumed future performance was based on past experience.

Another entrepreneur who benefited from solid financial projections is Ed Meltzer, the founder of Intelligent Wireless Systems of Prairie Village, Kansas. The company had developed radio frequency (RF) transceiver modules for the automation and control industry. Meltzer's research had pegged the market potential at $100 billion.

Intelligent Wireless had licensed the underlying technology and had gotten as far as it could in product development. Now Meltzer needed funds to complete development and roll out his first products.

The following summary projections are the ones Meltzer used to pitch to investors on his deal. During the latter half of 1997, Meltzer closed on approximately $500,000. The projections, as well as Meltzer's experience presenting them to investors, are used throughout this chapter to underscore key points.

◆ **Estimating sales for pre-revenue stage companies.** For companies that do not have revenues, such as Intelligent Wireless Systems, the act of projecting future sales is far more speculative than for companies with a track record. Fred Beste, a venture capitalist with NEPA Venture Funds, says, "It's naive to simply start with baseline sales and apply a formula that increases them by 20 percent per year. It's probably even more naive to suggest that the market is a certain size and that the penetration will increase a certain number of percentage points each year. The fact is, there's nothing formulaic whatsoever about projecting future sales. It requires going through the spreadsheet cell by cell and thinking about each quarter or month, and it's damn hard work."

The most effective sales projections for pre-revenue-stage

Summary Projected Operating Income, 1997–2000 Intelligent Wireless Systems

GROSS SALES, $	1997
49 MHZ PRODUCTS (4 PRODUCTS)	$1,762,500
ROUTER PRODUCTS (2 PRODUCTS)	273,500
TRANSPORTATION PRODUCT LINE (2 PRODUCTS)	170,000
2.4 GHZ PRODUCT LINE (2 PRODUCTS)	0
TOTAL SALES	2,206,000
COST OF SALES	1,313,801
GROSS MARGIN	892,199
SELLING, GENERAL, & ADMINISTRATIVE EXPENSES	778,671
INCOME FROM OPERATIONS	113,528

companies, he suggests, rely on some original market research or trial sales conducted by the founders. Neither of these activities needs to be exhaustive or expensive. However, they *do* need to get done. By doing so, the sales projections move out of the realm of fantasy and start moving into the world of reality.

At Intelligent Wireless Systems, Meltzer had an unfair advantage. Since the product technology was licensed from another firm that was fairly well known, Intelligent Wireless received a lot of inquires and even purchase orders for its products while they were in development. Even IBM called one day. Meltzer supplemented these inquiries with calls to buyers of RF products.

"We structured our questions very carefully," says Meltzer, "so that the answers, when taken together, would give us market research and some basis for estimating the sales we anticipated." Some questions Meltzer asked included: What is your time frame for purchasing RF products? What is the application? Is your project funded? Is there a scheduled launch? Is your application mission critical? How many units would you buy in a best-, or worst-case scenario?

When he added everything up, Meltzer had some 750,000 units he could sell in the first year. Incredibly, he

1998	1999	2000
$4,224,500	$10,192,500	$19,220,000
1,132,500	3,755,100	9,060,000
1,220,152	1,035,000	4,140,000
315,000	4,972,500	10,880,000
6,892,152	19,955,100	43,300,000
3,767,755	10,283,720	21,289,024
3,124,377	9,671,380	22,010,976
2,391,498	4,650,389	7,296,580
732,879	5,020,991	14,084,396

based his first-year revenues in 1997 on selling approximately 2 $^1/_2$ percent of what his research suggested—18,000 units—and throughout the five-year planning period never assumed he would hit more than 25 percent of what his research showed.

"That hurt and helped," recalls Meltzer. Ultra-conservative investors were pleased. "Others said, 'I'm not interested in a $40 million company, Ed, there's lots of those.'" At the end of the day, Meltzer was not conservative enough, at least for 1997. Raising the required funds took longer than expected so there was much less time in 1997 to hit even the conservative target.

◆ **Cost of goods sold.** Compared to sales, the cost of goods sold is much easier to work with. After all, while projected sales may require the business owner to consider where, when, and how long it will take to open new stores, the resulting cost of goods is a fait accompli because much of it relies on the thinking behind projected sales. When sales are known, the cost of sales is mostly plugging in numbers that you should be able to document.

However, good cost estimates work only if unit costs are known with some degree of certainty, which, for many companies, is a challenge that has to be met. The reason is simple. No one will invest in a company where not even the founder is sure what the cost will be to produce the product or service. *Would you?*

To get over this hurdle, Meltzer simply took his product design to the product manufacturer he knew he would be using and got a bill of materials from them. "They knew me," says Meltzer. "They knew I was a start-up and what they would be in for when we started ordering products." Meltzer took their prices and added in a fudge factor of 25 percent. "I took some heat for that one," says Meltzer. "But I ran a closely held family business for a long time using family money. When you do that, you're very conservative because you don't want to be wrong."

◆ **Gross margin.** In reality, though, the cost of goods sold is simply a means to the gross margin. Gross margin is defined as sales less cost of goods sold, and is usually expressed as a percentage. During the first and second glance, investors will probably pay more attention to the gross margin than the cost-of-goods-sold figure that produced it. What must the gross margin say or not say?

First, the gross margin should not be too far out of kilter with the gross margins that are earned in the industry at large. For instance, the National Restaurant Association reports that the gross margins for full-menu, table-service establishments are about 36 percent.

If you're opening a restaurant, and your financial projections show a 25 percent gross margin, up goes the red flag. If your projections show a 45 percent gross margin, up it goes again. While the former deviation is a tough sell, the latter is possible to overcome—but only with a plausible explanation.

In fact, a really good explanation is a selling point. Breakthroughs in technology, manufacturing techniques, or management styles can change the economics of doing business and create an exciting investment opportunity.

For instance, Abe Gustin Jr. and Lloyd Hill, co-chief executives of fast-growing Applebee's International, of Overland Park, Kansas, attribute restaurant dimensions to their superior margins. "The smaller size and seating capacity of our restaurants give us a distinct advantage over competing concepts, allowing us to open more restaurants in a given market and effectively draw customers from a smaller radius," they wrote in a letter to shareholders in a recent annual report. "In addition, greater market penetration increases our visibility . . . and increases the cost effectiveness of our marketing and advertising efforts."

Another important strategy regarding the projected gross margin is to pull back a bit from what might be suggested by the numbers alone. For instance, if the gross margin is 45 percent, it's wise to increase the cost of goods sold so that the gross margin in the projections is 42 percent or 43 percent instead. Why? Because a gross margin on a projected income statement is utopia. In real life there are strikes, stock-outs, equipment outages, and absenteeism. To add credibility to projected gross profits, build in a fudge factor of 2 percent to 3 percent.

◆ **Selling, general, and administrative expenses.** The easy part of this projection is the general and administrative costs. If ever there was a place in the projections to simply let costs increase each year by a factor, this is it. Supplies are not expensive. Calculating the cost of centralized operations, such as executive and administrative staff, is fairly straightforward.

Where companies go wrong is with the selling expenses, according to Peter Moore, a principal with Banking Dynamics, of Portland, Maine, a corporate financial consulting firm. Moore is also the founder of the Maine Investment Exchange, an angel investor forum. "Estimating selling costs can be one of the most challenging aspects of developing financial projections," he says, "because to do it right, entrepreneurs must be absolutely certain that their sales model works."

For products that have never been sold before, it's difficult to know this. Sometimes the projections indicate such. Moore says that entrepreneurs who suggest too many kinds of selling costs clue investors to the fact that they are uncertain how to sell their product or service.

Meltzer's selling costs for Intelligent Wireless were straightforward. He had line items for salespeople and advertising. "I knew that our product would lend itself to relationship selling, and that manufacturers' representatives couldn't do the job that we wanted."

◆ **Operating income, or the operating margin.** This is the famous bottom line, defined as gross income less selling, general, and administrative expenses.

It simply doesn't add to the understanding of the business or its value to project future gains and losses from extraordinary items, or for that matter, to project the tax liability on projected income. They defy any accurate prediction.

Many of the rules for better living on projected gross margins apply to the operating margins, as well. For instance, build in conservatism rather than extremism so that it's possible to exceed the projections rather than fall short of them.

Where operating margins exceed industry averages, have a tenable explanation of why. In the same way that technology, management style, and manufacturing techniques can cause a breakthrough on the gross margins, so, too, can paradigm shifts have a salubrious effect on operating margins.

For instance, Granite Financial, an equipment leasing company in Westminster, Colorado, enjoyed a near-vertical rise in revenues in its first 29 months in business and saw the opportunity to generate above-average operating margins. Why? According to vice president Rick Hilker, Granite's investments in connectivity technology with third-party sales organizations delivered significant operating leverage. "After a certain point," says Hilker, "we were able to handle large increases in lease volume with no increases in personnel costs on our end." Apparently, the strength of this reasoning delivered the goods and allowed Granite to consummate a $11.25 million initial public offering (IPO) during the fall of 1996.

For Meltzer, the percentage of the operating margin was of no particular concern because he was confident the company would be profitable, and he was not in an industry that had well-known ratios he would be expected to meet or exceed. "For me," he says, "they fell where they fell."

Happily, they fell well. In fact, the improvement in operating margins over time—from 5 percent to 32 percent—on improving gross margins and operating leverage, was, Meltzer reports, a good selling point for investors.

(To find out benchmarks for your industry on key financial ratios such as gross and operating margins, purchase a Statement Study from the banking trade organization Robert Morris Associates, Philadelphia, Pennsylvania; 215-446-4170 or 800-677-7621.)

Another important aspect of the operating margin is its absolute value. In general, if the operating margin as a percentage of sales is small, it's a turnoff for most investors. There is little room for error, and it's harder to create the kind of value that offers an exit for investors.

For many companies, however, thin margins are just part of the territory. However, when projected operating margins are thin because of a proposed low-cost pricing strategy, the credibility of an entrepreneur can be undermined.

If the underlying assumption is that profits come with volume, the questions become: Does the organization have the skill to generate the required volume? More important, what kind of cash (if there is any) is going to get eaten in inventory purchases and in carrying a large balance of accounts receivable that come part and parcel with a large sales volume?

 "You have to question the wisdom of an entrepreneur who is using a low-cost approach," says venture investor Beste. "In essence, they are using the one strategy that almost every competitor has at their disposal, but has simply chosen not to use yet."

The Importance of Historical Financial Statements in Raising Money

IT MAY SEEM ODD TO SAY, BUT THE FIRST STEP TOWARD making a good financial presentation is to *actually have historical financial statements*—one for each year the business has been in existence, or for the most recent five years. This would not seem to be worth mentioning were it not for the fact that producing a consistent set of historical financial statements seems to be an unusually challenging task for many entrepreneurs.

In addition, owners and managers of start-up companies are often prone to think they don't need financial statements because there's not much to put on them. This isn't necessarily the case.

First, if founders invested a lump of cash to get the business started, which is an extremely strong selling point, financial statements irrefutably document their commitment. Second, for founders who are working without pay or at less pay than to which they may otherwise be entitled, financial statements give them a place to document the company's growing liability to them.

Investors rarely pay off the company's debt to founders with their investment. They will, however, convert it to equity. However, generally speaking, if the owners' sweat equity is going to be a material part of the eventual negotiations, it needs to be out front and on the table from the beginning—which is exactly what happens when it's in the financial statements. It is also worth pointing out that to raise money, it borders on necessity that historical financial statements be prepared by a certified public accountant (CPA).

According to Rich Bendis, an angel who also is the executive director of the Kansas Technology Enterprise Corporation: "The presence of a CPA goes a long way toward assuring the investor—particularly angels—that what they are looking at is for real." Even if it's just a compilation, says Bendis, the investor knows the accountant's name is on it regardless, and nothing good can happen to his or her practice if the statements are inaccurate.

Even the lowest level of scrutiny offered by a CPA provides a high degree of comfort to investors. Certainly it provides the minimum level of comfort needed to get anyone from the outside to put money in the company.

◆ **Levels of accounting review and their importance.** Not every financial presentation requires a full-blown audit, according to Steven Mayer, a partner with the New York City–based accounting firm of Goldstein, Golub, Kessler, & Company. However, he says, there are other levels of review that lead up to an audit that are adequate for entrepreneurs in many instances.

"First, there's a compilation, in which the accounting firm creates financial statements out of the figures that are supplied by management," says Mayer. "In some cases, the accounting firm will simply retype numbers supplied to them by the company and might suggest the numbers appear reasonable," says Mayer.

The next level is generally known as an analytical review. "In addition to compiling the numbers that are supplied by management, some testing is done," Mayer says. Testing is not to measure financial performance, but to triangulate, to see that everything is lining up properly. "For example, if sales are up, and commissions are down, that's a strong signal that something may be very wrong with the way the numbers were put together," Mayer says.

The most intensive review that an accounting firm can

undertake is the audit. "Here," says Mayer, "in addition to all of the testing, third-party assurances are given that the figures presented are indeed accurate." This is why an audit takes so long. If a firm says it has, say, 25 personal computers for sale in its inventory, the auditor wants to see and count them. If the company says it has 25,000, the auditor wants to count them on a test basis. If the firm has 50 creditors, the auditor wants a letter from each verifying the amount. If 5,000, well, you get the picture.

Perhaps one of the most frequent occasions for an audit comes when you look for bank financing. According to Mayer, "At some loan level, the bank is going to want audited financial statements, and if you don't have them, you'll either need to get them or go packing." Though each bank is different, Mayer says that the minimum loan size that triggers the need for audited financial statements runs from $1 million to about $5 million.

Another reason for an audit, Mayer explains, is when absentee owners are involved in a business. Audited financial statements, because of the third-party assurances, can protect the absentee owner against fraud and mismanagement.

Public offerings also require a minimum of two years' audited financial statements. Firms on a fast-growth track often have their financial statements audited in anticipation of a future offering.

In addition, says Mayer, sometimes in private offerings the investors collectively will insist on audited financial statements. "Not only do the private-placement investors want assurances," he says, "they don't want anything to stand in the way of a public offering, which is often their 'exit strategy' or way of cashing out of the deal."

Mayer notes that an audit might start at $7,500. However, that would be for a service business in which there is no inventory to verify. If there are lots of inventory and receivables, then Mayer says there's almost no practical limit to how high the fees can run.

There is a commitment of time, as well. First, the accounting firm is going to camp out in your conference room for a couple of weeks. Because it's an audit, and because the accountant issues an opinion, and because there's loads of liability behind that opinion, the accountant might tend to be more conservative on certain matters—such as recognizing revenue—than you, as the paying client, are likely to be. "So you often spend time negotiating and reaching compromises on certain issues," says Mayer. "Frequently, it's a lot of time."

A Guided Tour of Historical Financials

SIMPLY HAVING FINANCIAL STATEMENTS CAN'T COMPLETELY carry the day, however. They've got to say the right things. To see how yours might measure up, take the following tour through a set of financial statements accompanied by Peter Ligeti, a general partner with Keystone Venture Capital Management Company, which finances companies from the so-called first stage and thereafter.

◆ **The income statement.** The first stop is the income statement, according to Ligeti. He says that "most investors look at gross, operating, and net margins to see if they are in line with industry averages." Next, they'll tend to look at the trends in contributions to revenues, if the company has more than one product or line. "Ideally," says Ligeti, "revenue figures will show a trend toward the higher margin products over time."

In addition, most investors will be looking at whether or not the revenues are recurring in nature—that is, are they coming from new or existing customers? "Obviously," says Ligeti, "it's much less expensive to generate revenues from existing customers than it is to go out and find new ones. If the revenue structure is a recurring one, it's easier to make the case for growing margins over time."

Next are the general and administrative expenses. "If these are high by industry standards," says Ligeti, "it's not necessarily a negative if you can make the case that you're simply managing income for tax purposes." After all, that's what small-business owners are supposed to do. However, general and administrative expenses pose a problem to investors, according to Ligeti, when the organization is top heavy.

Next, if research and development doesn't show up on the balance sheet in the form of capitalized expenditures, most investors will be looking for some R&D expenses to appear on the income statement. Of course, this mainly applies to technology companies, where innovation offers an edge. "R&D can be a very important factor for leading-edge-technology companies," says Ligeti, "because innovation is the force that will drive future revenues." At Intel, perhaps the penultimate technology company, the commitment to R&D is dramatic—it came in at $1.8 billion, or 8.6 percent of 1996 sales.

In addition to the overall volume of expenses, Ligeti says most equity investors also look at the trend relative to revenues. "They're looking for operating leverage. Ideally, the company is engaged in a business in which general and administrative expenses, as a percentage of sales, decrease as sales increase."

Operating leverage is a significant benefit, since under those conditions the company becomes more profitable, hence more valuable, the larger it gets. For example, Microsoft was able to deliver a $2.7 billion increase in revenues between fiscal 1995 and fiscal 1996, with an increase of just $811 million in selling, general, and administrative expenses. That's leverage.

Stepping back and looking at the income statement, Ligeti says an investor might wonder if a more conservative approach to accounting would turn what appears to be a profit into a loss. Deferred expenses, questionable gains or losses, and low returns and allowances charges relative to industry averages might all conspire to make the entire presentation look questionable. Better to get it all on the table for a candid evaluation than to appear as if you're trying to fool potential investors.

◆ **The cash-flow statement.** For an even closer look at how the company works, most investors will settle down with the cash-flow statement. Overall, they want to see how capital-intensive the business is (i.e., how many dollars have to be put into the business before one pops out).

"It's not that a capital-intensive business is bad," says

Ligeti. "It's simply that if a business needs lots of money, the equity investor needs to know it, because he or she is the person everyone is going to turn to as the business starts to experience growing pains."

For example, when analyzing the cash-flow statements for capital intensity, many investors will look for seasonality. Why? Seasonality eats cash because a business carries inventory that it cannot sell.

Another harbinger of capital intensity is lengthy collection periods. If these are combined with overall increases in the volume of receivables, it means that the company is getting squeezed. In fact, it's possible for a growth company to be highly profitable but have a cash flow that is negative every month.

"While receivables financing from banks would appear to alleviate some of the capital intensity, that's not always the case," Ligeti says. For new products, especially those that are technical in nature, there is uncertainty regarding their reliability and, as a result, market acceptance. In addition, services always make for funny receivables because there is no exchange of a physical product—nothing the seller can take back if the buyer fails to pay.

Because of these characteristics, service and growing technology companies often find receivables financing from banks difficult to find. "Oftentimes, it's the equity investor that has to fork over an extra layer of capital so that the operation can catch its breath," says Ligeti.

◆ **The balance sheet.** Next, investors might move over to the balance sheet. Unlike a banker, Ligeti says an equity investor is much less concerned with the presence of assets to liquidate if there are problems. "Whatever hard assets there may be are likely to be pledged to somebody else, anyway."

Most investors will zero in on the intangible assets. Whereas these don't mean boo to a lender, they speak volumes to an equity investor, especially for a technology-oriented company. For instance, if a company is capitalizing research and development (that is, treating expenditures for R&D as if they bought an asset), that's good, because it shows a significant commitment to product development and improvement, which may power future sales.

By the same token, if a company is too aggressive in its allocation of R&D expenditures to asset, rather than expense, accounts, it could be a negative. "A more conservative look at the income statement might cause a reclassification of expenditures as expenses and, in the process, deliver a big hit to earnings," says Ligeti, who recommends that companies adopt a clear policy on the capitalization versus the expensing of R&D expenditures.

Next, most investors will look at the inventory to see if it's in- or out-of-kilter with revenues. If the inventory account is high relative to the revenues or has been creeping up over time, it can give pause. "Maybe the company is gearing up for a big sale," says Ligeti. "But then again, maybe the company has poor management controls and is not responding to changes in its sales cycle."

Regarding accounts receivable, if there are any, many investors will take an interest in the revenue-recognition policies—that is, when during the sales cycle the firm actually books its revenues. In general, they're trying to see just how firm the revenues are reported by the company. "Growing businesses sometimes push sales out the door and book them right away, a policy that can be crippling with complex products or services that may take months to deliver to the satisfaction of the customer," says Ligeti.

Going over to the liabilities, Ligeti says that accounts payable can cause problems. Sometimes a $500,000 investment will get whittled down to $250,000 after the creditors stake their claim. "So important are the accounts payable," he says, "that investors may actually get on the phone to the creditors to see if they will hang in there a little longer." Entrepreneurs should be prepared to explain the precise amount of accounts payable that will be paid from the proceeds of the investment.

Moving down the liabilities, if there are any term loans, investors' comfort with them will vary directly with the length of the term. If it's two years, that could be a problem. If it's seven, that's much better.

Further down in the liabilities section, there are often

accrued salaries or "notes due founders." These can spell trouble for entrepreneurs who are not flexible. "Bankers simply subordinate these to their own debts and forget about them," says Ligeti. However, equity investors get a little prickly on this topic. "Basically, they don't want to end up paying off founders' loans."

Next, investors will look at the equity section of the balance sheet. They want to see if it's negative or positive. Remember, at the end of each year, the net income or net loss gets posted to the equity section of the balance sheet. If the company has been stringing together a series of losses, the equity will be pretty thin. If the equity account is negative, the company is technically insolvent. At the very least, it's running on fumes.

Finally, the investor will take a good look at the notes to the financial statements. "In fact," says Ligeti, "so important are the notes that some investors actually read them first. Notes to financial statements are just one more reason that CPA-prepared financial statements are essential. Internally generated financial statements rarely have them, handicapping investors and inviting them to walk away until notes become available."

CHAPTER 9

Preparing Business Plans

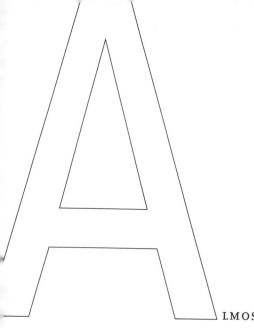

A LMOST EVERY REQUEST FOR equity financing begins with the same, seemingly innocuous request: "Send me your business plan." In a way, "business plan" is a misnomer. After all, it's not like anybody refers to a business plan every morning before deciding what to do that day.

First and foremost, the business plan is a *selling document*. It is a particularly difficult one to create because it must balance the unbridled enthusiasm of future prospects with the reporting of facts and details that are so important to investors.

Although every business and every business plan are different, the major sections of a successful plan are:

- ◆ Executive summary
- ◆ Description of the company and its business
- ◆ Market analysis
- ◆ Marketing operations

- Key personnel
- Financial analysis
- Appendices

Despite the blood, sweat, and tears that typically go into writing a business plan, investors frequently report that they never read them. For instance, Hans Severiens, an angel for 15 years and the coordinator of the Band of Angels, a group in San Francisco, says that he and most members of the band simply "skim through the plan."

Severiens's comment underscores an important point. Nobody ever raised money simply by *writing* a business plan. They raised money by *presenting* a business plan before investors. However, the latter cannot be done effectively without the former. Thus, writing the plan is really the blueprint for selling the deal.

This chapter provides an overview of the major

sections of a business plan. Rather than focusing on "how-to" aspects, it will help entrepreneurs overcome the common pitfalls of business plans that often cause investors to back off. In addition, this section provides entrepreneurs with the tools they will need to present their plan before investors, an exercise in which lasting impressions are made.

Questions Your Business Plan Should Answer

BY THE TIME YOU ARE FINISHED WRITING A BUSINESS PLAN, you should be able to persuasively answer the following 50 questions:

1 What is the price of your product or service, and why?
2 What are the company's existing products?
3 How much is the company worth?
4 How much capital is required to execute the expansion contemplated in the plan?
5 What is the use of proceeds?
6 On a summary basis, what is the historical financial performance of the company?
7 On a summary basis, what is the projected financial performance of the company?
8 What new products are being developed, and when will they be ready for market?
9 What is the size of the market for your product or service, in dollars?
10 What is the size of the market in terms of units?
11 How has the market for the product changed over the past five years, and why?
12 How do you anticipate the market will change going forward?
13 At what percentage rate is the market for your product growing?
14 Is the competition highly concentrated or highly fragmented?
15 What is your distribution channel, and why is it the best one?
16 If you are planning to advertise, in which publications? What are their circulations and frequencies, and why did you choose them?

17 How many people attend the trade shows at which you plan to exhibit?

18 What funding is being devoted to new product development, from financing and from ongoing operations?

19 How many potential customers have you talked to?

20 What is the gross margin on your product? Why is it superior or inferior to a competitor's?

21 What is your assumption on the collection period for outstanding receivables?

22 What are your working capital needs once sales take off, and how will these needs be addressed?

23 What will happen to gross and operating margins as sales rise, and why?

24 What percentage of your sales are recurring?

25 Who are your top five executives, and what is their professional and educational background?

26 What regulatory or legal threats are present?

27 Are there international markets for this product, and is the company positioned to take advantage of them?

28 Who is the largest competitor in your industry?

29 What criteria were used to choose locations for geographic expansion?

30 How will you get this product into mass-market distribution channels?

31 Is the product patented?

32 Who are your suppliers?

33 Do you have more than one supplier for each of your basic raw materials?

34 What are your payment terms with them?

35 What will cause gross and operating margins to improve as volume increases? Deteriorates?

36 Where is the company located, and how many square feet does it lease or own?

37 What is the length of the sales cycle?

38 How did you estimate returns and allowances?

39 How are sales personnel compensated? Incentivized?

40 What, as a percentage of sales, is the industry norm for annual R&D expenditures?

41 What is the earnings multiple of public companies like yours?

42 What are your immediate marketing objectives?

43 Does the company have a board of directors?

44 What is the ownership structure of the company? Who else is an owner?

45 How has the company been financed to date? What other financial transactions have occurred in the past three years?

46 Has the product generated any publicity? Where?

47 How many days old is the oldest current liability on the balance sheet?

48 Who has prepared the historical financial statements, and have they been compiled, reviewed, or audited?

49 Are sales cyclical?

50 What are the competitive advantages of your product(s)?

YOUR BUSINESS PLAN:

The Company and its Business

TRIEX GROUP INTERNATIONAL, A ONE-TIME MANUFACTURER of photoluminescent lighting products in San Leandro, California, was, after three years, insolvent, $500,000 in debt, and on its last legs. Oddly, an investor who met with management felt the situation held great promise. The investor's exact words were: "This company has great products. Obviously, the time and money consumed so far have been very well spent." The point of this story is that presenting a company's history is as important to securing capital as the future potential.

Ric Klass, an investment banker in New York City who concentrates on initial public offerings (IPOs) for emerging growth companies, explains, "Of course investors are buying into future potential," he says. "But in the present, they want to experience just two emotions: *comfort* that the business and the opportunity are for real, and *confidence* that the management team can pull it off."

Nothing delivers this emotional salve to investors better than tangible facilities, relationships, and actions by management. "When a business plan sells the future only and has nothing to report about the past or present, for me, it undermines the credibility of the company," says Klass.

The following is a list of 10 items that could go into this section of the plan that build credibility. Some are quite obvious entries for established companies; others are creative suggestions for earlier-stage companies that don't have much history to bank on. Note, also, the large numbers of names and telephone numbers that are suggested for inclusion. The tacit agreement is that these contacts are fair game for the investor's due diligence. Though investors rarely call contacts out of the blue, the offer of so many contacts increases the investor's comfort because it shows how many other business people have confidence in the company.

1 **History or time line.** This should cite key accomplishments and critical milestones. This can be particularly helpful to "virtual" companies, not yet incorporated, with the founders perhaps holding down other, full-time jobs.

2 **List of important assets.** Make known your patents, service marks, trademarks, copyrights, proprietary software, or databases.

3 **Description of facilities.** Remember, details are important because they provide comfort. Therefore, if facilities are leased, include price, lease expiration, square footage, and special features such as elevated floors, security, and proximity to vendors.

4 **List of suppliers.** If there are too many, list the top 25 with name, address, telephone number, contact name, and approximate volume of business.

5 **Professional advisers.** Lawyers and accountants are the obvious choices. However, add in any other consultants who have been used in the past year, plus the names of members of your advisory board or your board of directors.

6 **Strategic partners.** Formal or informal relationships with other firms, individuals, or organizations all put meat on the bones. Examples include the names of manufacturers' representatives, independent agents selling the product or service, and joint-venture partners.

7 **Operations.** A review of your operations shows how the product is made or the service is offered.

8 **Customer lists.** If there are too many, supply profiles of representative customers. Also, for relationship-based cus-

tomers, get permission to include their names and telephone numbers and ask them to expect calls.

9 **Market studies.** The actual results and analyses belong elsewhere in the plan. But the fact that management conducted studies, and the way they did so, are particularly effective confidence builders for early-stage companies to provide.

10 **Description of products and services.** That a description of the company's products and services is just a part of the picture indicates how much there is to the company. It underscores the point that, to investors, a company is much more than simply the products it sells, or says it will sell.

YOUR BUSINESS PLAN:

Market Analysis

VENTURE CAPITALIST TED SCHLEIN, OF KLEINER, PERKINS, Caufield & Byers, says that when he gets a business plan he looks for just three things: "Do you have a market? Does your product address it? Do you have a team that can get the product into the market?"

The first and most fundamental question is: Is there a market for your product or service? If your analysis cannot answer this question, then many investors simply have no interest in the answers to the second and third questions. The items that a market analysis should contain include:

◆ Estimate of market size
◆ Estimate of growth rates
◆ Macroeconomic factors driving sales or creating opportunity
◆ Microeconomic factors driving sales or creating opportunity
◆ Description and analysis of competitors
◆ Description of competitive advantages.

It's not just venture capital investors who maintain this attitude. Bill Simms, an angel in Sacramento, California, who invests both for his own account and for a Fortune 500 corporation, says that he continues to "turn down deals where the company founders are unable to articulate what the market opportunity is, and how they fit into it."

It is an act of courage to go against the grain of the universally useful "keep-it-simple" doctrine, but necessary for an effective market analysis. Venture capitalist Schlein says that entrepreneurs are not credible when they suggest that a market is a certain size and they seek a certain percentage penetration. "As a typical example, an entrepreneur will tell me they want to do Java online games because it's a huge market with all those modems out there," says Schlein. "But they aren't credible because they haven't found out how many of these modems are faster than the minimum 28k speed their product will require."

Simplified approaches to market analysis don't work because markets are rarely uniform. For any product or service there is a wide range of buying behaviors and preferences, which a single source can rarely accommodate.

MARKET ANALYSIS: A CASE IN POINT

AN EXCELLENT EXAMPLE OF MARKET DEFINITION AND SEGmentation came from Energy Brands, Inc., a Whitestone, New York, beverage company whose major product line at the time it drafted a business plan was bottled water.

The overall market dimensions were quickly supplied by Beverage Marketing Corporation, a research firm in New York City. Gallonage for bottled water had grown at a compound annual rate of 10 percent, and by 1995 stood at 2.8 billion gallons. Wholesale dollar sales had grown at 8.4 percent compounded annually since 1985, and by 1995 stood at $3.4 billion.

However, to say that Energy Brands would capture 1, 2, 5, or even 10 percent of this market was too simple because of differences among buyers. More important, if Energy Brands stayed within the rigid confines of this definition, the company would lose an important selling point for its deal. By looking at the situation more carefully, Energy Brands could help investors see a much different, and much brighter, picture.

In truth, the office segment of the market, sold in five-gallon units, was stable. So, too, were sales of spring water sold in one-gallon units through the supermarket channel.

However, what was red-hot at the time, growing at a compound annual growth rate of 25 percent per year, was bottled water sold in containers of 1.5 liters or less through the convenience and gourmet distribution channel.

By segmenting their market this way, Energy Brands' management had a *story* to tell. Bottled water in convenience sizes, they told investors, had been astutely packaged so that it could be sold as an alternative beverage to soda, New Age teas, and juices. Health- and purity-conscious American consumers were taking the bait in unprecedented volumes, as the sales figures demonstrated.

Now, investors could understand the current dimensions of the market, but they could also see that it would continue to expand as water stole share from other beverage categories. In addition, the market segmentation helped management make the case for the packaging and brand-related expenditures that the plan called for. Suddenly, Energy Brands's business plan made sense. The market analysis showed investors that preconceived notions about selling water had changed, and that the management of Energy Brands, Inc. was clearly onto something.

Unfortunately, a good market analysis is not something that business owners can simply talk their way through; it must be supported by original research and/or third-party sources. As venture capital investor Schlein says, "The absence of detail is a possible kiss of death."

It is easy to see why. Without it, entrepreneurs are simply talking off the tops of their heads. They might really know what they are talking about. However, if investors don't know an entrepreneur well, they might start to think, "Why should I believe him or her?"

Remember, the investor is looking for just two things: *comfort* and *confidence.* In this context, nothing builds comfort more than an authoritative, third-party source supporting the conclusions of the business plan. Going out and finding this stuff is one of the necessary evils of the process.

YOUR BUSINESS PLAN:

Marketing Operations

BUILD A BETTER MOUSETRAP AND THE WORLD WILL BEAT A
path to your door—a statement that may actually be accurate.

But the rest of the story is that not nearly enough people
will actually *buy* your mousetrap that you can generate earnings growth of 25 percent per year. Not without some first-
rate marketing, at least.

The marketing-operations section of the plan must go
beyond an analysis that illuminates the opportunity. It must
also point to specific strategies and tactics that tell investors
how the company will capitalize on it. For the majority of
emerging companies, future marketing operations is the
heart of the plan because it describes the activities upon
which future success will rest.

"Unfortunately," says Ron Conway, a private investor in
Atherton, California, and a member of San Francisco's Band
of Angels, "the marketing [operations] section of the plan is
also the downfall of companies raising money because it
often reveals a lack of sophistication about how sales are
actually made and product is moved."

The following are some traps to avoid in describing your
marketing operations:

◆ **The vice president of sales.** Company founders make a
serious mistake in their business plan by suggesting that
future operations will consist of hiring a vice president of
sales. There may, someday, be a vice president of sales. "But
to get enthusiastic about a company," says Conway, "I need
to see a vision and a strategy for how they are going to get
their product into the market." The problem with the vice
president of sales is that it leaves open the question of
whether or not there is a vision and a strategy to begin with.
The equity investor is investing in *you*, not someone that you
might hire.

◆ **Too many marketing devices.** Another way that entrepreneurs turn off investors is by suggesting that the company
will utilize several marketing devices. What this frequently
tells investors is that the company really doesn't have a clue

how to sell the product.

A not uncommon gaffe reads: "Upon financing, the company will engage in an integrated program of sales and marketing encompassing direct selling through manufacturers' representatives, the creation of a company sales force, trade advertising, direct mailing, trade-show promotion, telemarketing, and networking."

This problem becomes apparent in the financial statements as well, when forecasted selling expenses reflect too many line items. According to financing consultant Peter Moore, founder of Banking Dynamics, as well as the Maine Investment Exchange: "It doesn't matter if the problem shows up on the financial statements or the marketing-operations section of the plan. When the investor sees you do not have a cohesive sales model, your chances of raising

Sales Tactics and Market Research

	PRINT ADVERTISING	CONSUMER PRODUCT IN MASS MARKET CHANNELS
A SIMPLIFIED APPROACH TO SALES TACTICS	Outbound telemarketing to uncover leads and set appointments, followed by direct selling to representatives.	Utilize manufacturers to gain shelf space, stimulate in-store demand with cooperative advertising.
LOW-COST MARKET RESEARCH TEST	Call 200 prospects, record number of appointments.	Interview 12 buyers working for target retailers, get estimates on demand, and information on cooperative advertising opportunities.

capital will be undermined."

Naturally, established companies have a sales model developed from experience. However, for companies that are raising capital to commence marketing, the best bet for inspiring confidence among investors is to suggest a simplified approach with moving parts that can be tested.

For example in 1980, giant Software Publishing Corp. was looking for $250,000 in equity financing to ramp up sales for its PC software. At the time, the market for its products was just $350 million. The company's business plan boiled down its marketing strategy to a one-two punch. Specifically, the company used advertising to *pull* consumers into retail stores and point-of-purchase displays to *push* the product once consumers got there.

The beauty of applying this kind of logic to a business

RESTAURANT DINING	PROFESSIONAL SERVICES FOR CONSUMERS	HIGH TECH PRODUCT
Saturation mailings in a three-mile radius promoting discounts, followed by in-house promotions to stimulate repeat business.	Short-form television coordinated with inbound telemarketing.	Direct selling by company-paid salespeople combined with direct mail to create a continuous flow of warm leads.
Hand-deliver 1,000 flyers within three-mile radius and record response.	Get response rates for similar programs that are published in trade literature. Produce low-budget infomercial run on public access cable slots.	Interview 25 potential customers and report buying protocols. Send out 1,000 direct mailers, and record response.

plan is that it breaks the marketing operations down to a limited number of tasks that can be described with the kind of authority and detail that offers investors comfort. More important, as the market research section of the chart indicates, this approach gives the entrepreneur the opportunity to conduct marketing operations on a test basis and make claims based on experience rather than supposition.

YOUR BUSINESS PLAN:
Key Personnel

WHILE THE MAJORITY OF INVESTORS SAY THEY NEVER READ business plans cover-to-cover, they all refer to certain sections they consider critical. Though the precise sections vary from investor to investor, the discussion of key personnel always rises to the top of the list.

Retired admiral Bobby Inman, an angel investor, says that when he gets a business plan, he first tries to determine if it's a field he's interested in. "But then I immediately turn to the key-personnel section of the plan," he says.

Ted Schlein, a venture capitalist with Kleiner, Perkins, Caulfield & Byers, concurs with Inman's approach to reading business plans. "As a general rule," he says, "I don't read the business plan cover-to-cover. But I do look at the team almost right away, because I want to see what right they have to make the claims they are making in the plan."

Why do Inman and Schlein, like every other equity investor, turn to the personnel section of the business plan first? Human nature. Investors want to know who is running the company and how many degrees of separation are between these people and themselves.

For some investors, a connection to management—no matter how thin—is vital to getting the process to the next step. However, sooner or later the attention focuses on the men and women at the helm of the company and their qualifications. After all, like the old real-estate mantra—location, location, location—the entrepreneurial finance mantra is management, management, management. For better or for worse, however, the first time an investor meets management is often the biographical sketches in the business plan.

"When I read the biographies of the people running the company, there are a number of things I'm looking for," says Inman. "Is this their idea, or are they executing someone else's? If it's someone else's idea, I generally decline. Are the founders at great personal risk with this venture? Have they put in all the capital they can? Have they ever been through a downsizing and worked with scarce resources to create success? Naturally, each situation is different, but these are some of the benchmark experiences I look for."

The following is a model biographical sketch of a business owner that founded a successful long-distance reseller. This entrepreneur was looking for several million dollars to roll out Internet access services to her existing client base. The fictional names for this real person and real company are Betty B. Good and BBG Telecommunications.

Ms. Betty B. Good, president and chief executive officer, founded and capitalized the company with her own savings in 1990. Initially, she served as the operations manager and primary salesperson for the company. However, upon reaching monthly sales of one million minutes in 1991, Ms. Good recruited, hired, and trained a vice president of sales and a vice president of operations. From 1991 to 1994, Ms. Good was primarily responsible for business development. In this capacity she negotiated long-term contracts with major facilities-based, long-distance carriers and reduced BBG's average cost per minute by more than 70 percent. Though this was accomplished during a period of declining prices, the cost advantage that BBG currently maintains over several competitors is testimony to her negotiating skills. During this period, Ms. Good also led the company's successful entry into switch-based telecommunications, which lowered overall operating costs for the company and introduced a new revenue center. Since 1995, Ms. Good has been principally involved in planning the company's expansion into new telecommunication services. In this capacity she forged strategic alliances with several key vendors, and recruited additional managerial and executive personnel to assist in the company's planned rollout of Internet-access services. Prior to forming the company, Ms. Good was vice president of marketing for Rival Communications. There, she managed the company's direct-marketing efforts, and was responsible for 300 telemarketers with 12 regional managers reporting directly to her. During her tenure there, Rival sales grew by more than 22 percent annually. Prior to joining Rival, Ms. Good was an account representative for AT&T Business Services Group, where she sold advanced telecommunications services to middle-market businesses. Ms. Good earned her bachelor's degree in English from Boston College.

Clearly, another challenge companies raising money face is an incomplete management team. The best way to overcome this shortfall is to acknowledge it in the business plan. In fact, the very act of saying in effect, "I am going to surround myself with smarter people than me as we grow," tends to increase the currency of the entrepreneur.

Your best bet is to confess management deficits up front and create biographical profiles of the talent you *will* need. A well-conceived business plan will offer readers a description of the ideal candidate, including experience, critical skills, and educational background. Most important, the biographical sketch will detail the tasks and responsibilities of this individual.

By sketching out the successful candidate, business owners are telling investors they won't pass important responsibilities to just anyone. Instead, they have considered beforehand the skills and experience required in key positions in order for the business to succeed.

On a somewhat grander scale, another successful technique for inspiring confidence is to provide organizational charts for management in each of the years covered by the financial projections in the business plan. Again, by offering critical thinking rather than open-ended declarative statements, entrepreneurs inspire the confidence of investors.

Finally, include biographical sketches for the board of

directors and for an advisory board (if there is one) to increase the connection your company has with the potential investor.

Financial Analysis

THE BULK OF THE FINANCIAL ANALYSIS SECTION OF THE business plan consists of historical and projected financial statements. This was covered in detail in Chapter 8. As a result, the balance of this section lists the other items that should be included in the financial analysis section of the plan, along with advice about how to make the most of them.

◆ **Summary valuation analysis.** The development of a valuation analysis was covered in Chapter Seven. A summary valuation spreadsheet should be included in the financial-analysis section of the business plan, though its presence is somewhat controversial.

One school of thought says that putting a value on the company is a mistake because it will turn off many investors before they have been romanced by the business, the products, or the management. The other school says to seize the initiative and tell the investors what you feel the business is worth. If buyers really want something, they won't walk away simply because they disagree with the price.

The best advice is tell investors the valuation you are placing on the business because early in the game they are looking for guidance on the answer to this question. However, your valuation must be *reasonable*; if it's not, you could blow it then and there.

◆ **Summary projected and historical financial statements.** It is always a good idea to put *summary* projected and historical financial data in the financial analysis section of the plan (before the full-blown financials) as a simple convenience. Many times investors want to zoom out and look at the big picture, rather than get caught up in the minutia of monthly cash-flow statements. When investors put down the business plan to summarize things later, because there's no time at the present, they may never pick it up again.

The projected and historical financials can be summarized with five lines. These are 1) revenues; 2) cost of sales; 3) gross profit; 4) selling, general, and administrative expenses; and 5) operating profit. Create one summary for historical performance and another one for projected performance.

◆ **Use of Proceeds.** Most investors are used to seeing short "Use of Proceeds" charts that are standard in prospectuses. A business plan, however, should go one level of organization deeper. Thus, while one line item might read "Marketing: $300,000," a well-written business plan will provide a little more support. Under "Marketing: $300,000," it will also offer "Sales Personnel: $150,000" and "Direct Response: $150,000."

◆ **Assumptions to financial projections.** The credibility of the business plan at large hinges on how well the front of the book, which describes the business, meshes with the back of the book, which estimates future financial performance.

For instance, if the marketing operations section of the plan calls for territorial expansion in Year 3, complete with satellite manufacturing facilities, then Year 3 of the financial projections must reflect these expenditures. Similarly, unit costs described in the company- and product-descriptions section of the business plan must mesh with the costs of goods sold.

The most effective way to accomplish this seamless bonding is to have a well-documented set of assumptions to the financial projections. In the flora and fauna of a business plan, the projections are somewhat of a hybrid mutation. They are not quite numerical, but then they are not quite descriptive prose, either. However, the act of spelling out the many variables and formulas of the financial projections makes it easier to integrate their implications into the rest of the plan.

For instance, the assumption that "advertising equals 9 percent of sales" provide a budget around which several aspects of the marketing operations section of the plan can be built. Likewise, the assumption that "each five new stores opened will require a dedicated manager, and each 20 stores opened will require a regional manager" makes it much easier to create projected organizational charts.

Appendices

APPENDICES BUILD THE CONFIDENCE OF INVESTORS AS THEY read a business plan. After all, it's the place where companies can show something that is real. Here's a list of items that companies can put in the appendices of their business plans, with a brief description of the mileage they earn for doing so.

◆ **Product literature.** Shows the product is for real. Provides insight into the caliber of management's thinking and execution on marketing communications.

◆ **Patents.** Indisputable proof of patent protection. Demonstrates foresight.

◆ **Company-sponsored research.** Obviously, few emerging companies have the resources to hire professional survey firms, but every firm can take the temperature of the market in one way or another. Even transcripts from interviews with potential customers demonstrate that management bases its planning on reality rather than supposition.

◆ **Sample sales contracts and agreements.** Shows that the firm is ready to make sales and has considered some of the legal implications of selling the product or service.

201

◆ **Publicity.** Provides third-party verification of the company's activities. Shows the company and/or its products are favorably received by a critical and unbiased audience.

◆ **Trade articles.** Provides additional support for the company's claims regarding market trends and sizes.

◆ **Advertising concepts.** For electronic media, sample scripts with rudimentary storyboards; for print media, copy and rough visuals. Demonstrates the company has considered the positioning of its products. Provides greater validity to the claim that the company will utilize advertising to stimulate sales. Offers additional evidence that the company is in a state of readiness to commence marketing activities.

◆ **Supporting financial schedules.** Items such as additional detail on cost-of-goods calculations, bills of material, the anatomy of profit earned on a single sale increase the investor's feeling that the financial projections are based in reality.

- ◆ **Licenses and permits.** Shows the company is law-abiding and will not experience an interruption of operations at the hands of regulatory authorities.
- ◆ **References.** The contact names, addresses, and telephone numbers of selected customers, key suppliers, and professional advisers will increase the sense of cooperation the investor feels. They will also increase the perceived level of managerial talent.
- ◆ **Customer testimonials.** The oldest trick in the book, for good reason.
- ◆ **Graphics.** Pictures of facilities, manufacturing, sites, maps, and engineering drawings add to credibility.

There are no hard and fast rules about what to put into the appendices of a business plan because each company has its own unique story to tell. The general theory, though, is to include items that increase the credibility of the company with investors.

As a final note, it's important to make clear separations between different appendices. The many elements that can go into appendices are graphically and visually disparate. When presented without the "editing" of cover sheets or separations, the effect is more confusing than enlightening.

YOUR BUSINESS PLAN:

Executive Summary

WRITE THE EXECUTIVE SUMMARY LAST. AT THAT POINT, IT'S the easiest part of the plan to write because all of the hard thinking is already done. It is also the most *important* part of the business plan.

Again, most investors don't read business plans cover-to-cover. However, most will force themselves to read the executive summary. Hans Severiens, coordinator for the Band of Angels, says, "When I get a business plan, I look at the people, the executive summary, and the market analysis. I use the executive summary to decide whether or not to go any further with the company."

Kleiner, Perkins' Ted Schlein concurs. "I look at the executive summary first. If the company cannot explain what they are doing in two to three pages, it's very difficult for me to get interested."

Schlein's comment underscores one of the most important features about an executive summary: *length*. Highly detailed and lengthy executive summaries are not generally effective. If the executive summary is presented on two pages, however, investors can absorb everything at one glance. Boiling a venture down to this length should not be hard, since the executive summary need only recap the major sections of the plan. In fact, if the plan is really wired tight, it's simply a matter of lifting sentences from the body of the plan and stringing them together.

The only section in the executive summary that is not lifted verbatim from the body of the plan is something called a *Summary Statement*. This summary statement is the first paragraph an investor reads about the company. It is similar to the preface of a book which provides a reader with context and perspective; it tells investors why they need to read the rest of the plan. However, unlike a preface, which can run many pages, a summary statement must do its work in a single paragraph and must do it well enough to capture the imagination of readers, keeping them interested in reading.

The following is a sample summary statement from a business plan that ultimately raised more than $1 million.

Dermaceutical Labs, Inc. has developed and markets a line of revolutionary anti-aging and skin-care products marketed under the brand name NuCelle®. The moment for a line of products like NuCelle® is now. Several demographic and attitudinal shifts—an aging population, rising importance of physical appearance, growing concern over skin-related disease and consumer acceptance of alpha hydroxy-based products—are delivering double-digit increases in the market for cosmetic products sold through direct-response channels. The management of DLI believes that with an equity capital infusion, NuCelle® can capture the full potential of opportunities which are now emerging in the $200 billion market for cosmetics. Dermaceutical Labs estimates that the programs and strategies outlined in this plan will generate sales and net income of $27 million and $2.5 million, respectively, during the first 12 months following funding.

As a parting comment, remember that the executive summary is the section of the plan investors will read first. If investors like what they read in the summary, meet with management, and get turned on, the rest of the deal might get negotiated without the plan ever getting read in its entirety. If, however, investors cannot make it through the summary, the plan has failed to help achieve the ultimate objective, and the rest of the plan is for naught.

Do not be discouraged, though. Many nos are required to get to yes. And you didn't waste any time preparing the plan. The analysis, planning, and downright hard, analytical thinking that went into the document will pay dividends for a long time to come.

Presenting Your Business Plan

ONE OF THE MAIN PURPOSES OF WRITING A BUSINESS PLAN is to prepare entrepreneurs to present and defend it before investors. Even if investors never read the many sentences you fervently wrestled to the ground, no time was wasted. Such efforts prepare you for the presentation.

The discipline of presenting a business plan to investors is beyond the scope of this work. However, this section provides the framework for presenting to investors, as well as a list of dos and don'ts.

Presenting a business plan to investors is roughly the same whether the group is large or small and regardless of whether the investors are angels, investment bankers, or venture capitalists. The presentation must, in 20 minutes, answer the following five questions:

1 What is the company and what are its strengths?
2 How has it performed?
3 Where is it going?
4 How is it going to get there?
5 What does it mean for investors if they succeed?

To do this, entrepreneurs must cover the same functional areas as their business plan. Specifically:

1 Summary
2 Description of the company and its business
3 Market analysis
4 Marketing operations/expansion plan
5 Key personnel
6 Financial analysis

Perhaps the nation's leading authority on investor presentations, by sheer numbers alone, is Jeffery Adduci, president of the Regional Investment Bankers Association (RIBA), of Charleston, South Carolina. The RIBA is a trade association which, among other activities, hosts five investment banking presentations per year for companies seeking an investment banker, selling an initial public offering (IPO), or developing market support. During his tenure with the group, Adduci has run 50 conferences, and as a result has seen 1,600 presentations by companies raising money.

"I have not only seen these presentations, but have the context of perspective," he says. "By far, the most successful companies at raising money are those whose management is effective at presenting themselves." Here are Adduci's observations on areas where companies frequently go wrong:

◆ **Poor timing.** "Entrepreneurs frequently say too much or don't say enough. Either extreme is deadly," according to Adduci. When the presentation is too long, it puts investors to sleep, indicating the entrepreneur is unsophisticated about the rules of engagement and uncertain what information is important to investors. When the presentation is too short, the entrepreneur appears to be unwilling to share important information. The right length for your presentation is 20 minutes; 25, if your company is the next Microsoft.

◆ **Live demonstrations.** These are almost always a failure, particularly for technology-based products.

Adduci recalls one conference where a company attempted a live, online demonstration. The screen on the speaker's laptop was projected onto a large screen at the front of the auditorium so that the 175 investment bankers in the room could see what was happening. "The entrepreneur took the podium and hit the magic start button on his laptop computer," recalls Adduci. "Unfortunately, the response was an error message indicating the Internet connection was broken."

The speaker tried to log back on while introducing himself and the company. When the second attempt failed, the great elixir of personal computing—rebooting—was applied. Unfortunately, this threw the large-screen projector, and threw it terribly, causing the large-screen image to disintegrate into a sickly rainbow. The audiovisual staff began to scramble, but it was too late—the damage had been done.

Your best bet: Use videotape for perfect demonstrations every time.

◆ **Suspect numbers.** Many times entrepreneurs present historical profits which, upon further and perhaps more conservative examination, might actually indicate a loss. Others will present growth curves that look like a hockey stick. Aggressive revenue-recognition policies, unrealistic reserves for returns or bad debts, overzealous capitalization of expenditures, the presence of deferred expenses—all of these turn profits into losses, and all work against companies. "When outrageous numbers show up on the overheads," says Adduci, "I've noticed that's when investors leave the room."

◆ **Droning on about technology.** "Entrepreneurs who are scientists or engineers are prone to make this error," according to Adduci. It hurts, he says, because "once you lose investors' attention, it can be hard to get it back." Granted, the technical aspects of companies' products or services are important, inasmuch as they deliver competitive advantages, open new markets, or change the balance of power in an existing one. To investors, however, technology is not important in and of itself.

Spend no more than three to five minutes discussing technology. Any more time spent on science is less time devoted to selling the deal.

◆ **Poor attitude.** A banker might tolerate a fractious borrower. After all, if the company can repay a loan, the company can repay a loan. Equity investors are different, however. In many ways they are partners, and nobody wants a partner who will not listen to them. Adduci says, "Entrepreneurs who come across as condescending, unhelpful, rude, or above it all tend to be less successful than those who are engaging."

◆ **Poor response to questions.** "Many entrepreneurs goof on the inevitable question-and-answer part of the program," says Adduci. There are many ways to do this. The most damaging, however, occurs when entrepreneurs give the impression that they're smarter than the person asking the question and compound their error by throwing lots of technical jargon into the answer. It's best to repeat questions before answering them and give investors an opportunity to verify that you have repeated it correctly.

◆ **Inappropriate audiovisual support.** "It's a mistake to let a corporate video run on for more than five minutes," says Adduci. "After that amount of time, it starts to give investors the impression that management is trying to hide something."

At the same time, he says, making a presentation with no visual support whatsoever is difficult for all but the most gifted of speakers. The reason? "With so little time to say so much, if investors get distracted for even a moment, they may lose the context of the speaker's remarks without a visual outline," he says. The most effective presentations are accompanied by 10 to 15 slides, overheads, or handouts that punctuate the speaker's remarks and that give listeners a constant source of context. The slides on pages 208 and 209 were used in presentations by Cooperative Images, Inc., a company that helps physicians market elective surgical procedures. The company was successful in raising $300,000.

◆ **Inappropriate follow-up.** When raising capital, particularly through private investors, the old rule is that "yes comes fast, and no takes forever." Still, many investors will test the mettle of business owners by seeing how long it takes them to follow up. If it's not forthcoming, even for reasons of courtesy, many investors get turned off. On the other side of the coin, calling every day doesn't work either.

Follow up rapidly, but no more than three times. Then wait. If you haven't gotten an answer in two weeks, write the investor off and move on.

◆ **Burning bridges.** Raising money often takes a long, long time. Adduci has seen companies come to his conferences over the course of two years. Sometimes the things that

①

SUMMARY
◆ Provides marketing services to physicians
◆ Formed two years ago, profitable
◆ Formed Elective Investments starting 1997
◆ Elective Investments finances procedures generated by Cooperative Images

②

THE TRANSACTION
◆ Loan
◆ Equity Kicker
◆ Proceeds earmarked for sales expansion and sales expansion only
◆ Liquidity for equity investors

③

THE OPPORTUNITY
◆ Historical focus on wealthy customers—2% market
◆ We have tapped the other 60% of the market who can afford it, just not all at once
◆ Trend toward capitation of fees is creating competition in elective surgical market

④

OPERATIONS
◆ Solicit physicians, win contracts
◆ Regional direct response TV marketing
◆ Dunn Communications
◆ Outbound telemarketing
◆ Quality leads, set appointments

⑤

MILESTONES
◆ Selling to physicians
◆ Generating consumer inquiries
◆ Effective management of telemarketing while maintaining a professional and ethical sales process
◆ Importance of patient financing

⑥

ELECTIVE INVESTMENTS
◆ Historical approval rates have been low
◆ Agreement with Travelers Investment Corp. and Financial Resources, Inc.
◆ Others being negotiated—*Wall Street Journal* ad
◆ Delivers new profit center

⑦

soured investors who saw the deal early on—product not fully developed, no sales, incomplete management team—correct themselves during the fund-raising process. "Contacts made early on may at some point become fertile ground for raising capital," he says, "unless, of course, the entrepreneur hasn't kept in touch, or worse yet, was less than gracious when the investor said 'no thanks' the first time around."

COMPETITIVE ADVANTAGES OFFERED BY ELECTIVE INVESTMENTS
- Increases number of qualified patients
- Increases length of contract with physicians
- Creates homogeneous pool of consumer debt

(8)

KEY PERSONNEL
- Gerry Powell— Chapel Creek Enterprises
- Charlie Lynn
- Vincent Trapasso

(9)

HISTORICAL, PROJECTED PERFORMANCE

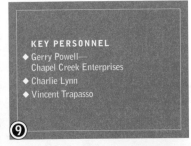

	1995	1996	1997	1998	1999
Contracts	12	30	91	175	259
Contract Rev. (000)	$231	852	4,463	10,828	17,632
Operating Inc. (000)	($32)	88	853	4,100	7,760
Notes Withstanding (#)	0	0	3,400	8,928	12,048
Gain on Sale of Notes (000)	$0	0	850	2,232	3,012
Operating Inc. (000)	$0	0	473	1,580	1,730

(10)

INVESTMENT CONSIDERATIONS
- Proven operations and concept
- Growing market
- Skilled management with history of growing innovative businesses
- Flexible financing

(11)

Conclusion

NOW WHAT?

IN THE FACE OF SO MUCH INFORMATION, IT'S OFTEN difficult to know what your first step should be.

That's easy. Start talking. Don't commit yourself to any particular course of action, such as going public or raising venture capital.

Simply start talking with business people who know you well and whom you respect, and tell them you are considering raising capital. Listen to what they say and see where they point you. Challenge their ideas with the knowledge you have absorbed from this book.

Next, get out from behind your desk. You cannot raise outside capital by staying inside. The "Resources" section of this book offers several venture capital clubs and forums worth attending. Go. Talk. Listen. Will you come back with a check? Probably not. However, you will know where to turn when you formally commence your search.

Then, start writing your business plan. My firm is frequently asked to write these plans, and entrepreneurs want to know how long this will take. The answer is always the same. No matter how fast we write, it will not happen in less than 45 days, and might take as long as 180. The reason is that writing the plan provokes all kinds of thorny issues that must be settled and sometimes requires the benefit of lengthy analysis and consideration. These issues range from engineering to sales and sometimes, at the most fundamental level, to the form of incorporation.

Start this process now for the reasons mentioned above, and because luck is where opportunity and preparation meet.

Finally, start planning. I believe that planning is hard to do, especially for entrepreneurs. Work toward assembling all of the fundamental pieces you need. Get historical financial statements. Line up references who will speak on your behalf. Complete your business plan. Rehearse your pitch to investors. Start generating leads.

Raising the capital you require will take you

through a gamut of emotions, ranging from discouragement to exhilaration. One of its enduring charms, however, is the people you meet along the way. Equity investors are different, especially at this stage of the game. They are really partners. They meet with you in expectation of perhaps sharing a common goal. They know that your success could be their success, and therefore they ultimately want to see you win.

Resources

Appendix A
PRIVATE EQUITY CAPITAL DIRECTORY

THE FOLLOWING LIST OF VENTURE CAPITAL CLUBS AND NETWORKS
will help entrepreneurs locate equity capital from individual investors. There are noteworthy differences between venture capital clubs and networks. Clubs foster interaction between entrepreneurs and investors, generally with some educational component. Networks, on the other hand, strive to match entrepreneurs and investors based on an analysis of key variables, such as industry, stage of development, and the amount of capital required.

Many metropolitan areas boast venture capital clubs that cater *exclusively* to venture capital funds and the professionals who manage them. These clubs and organizations were not included in this directory. Only the many venture capital organizations that cater to individuals are listed.

The distribution of clubs and networks is not even. Some states have more activity than others. Generally, the level of venture capital club activity is directly proportional to the number of technology companies in a state because they create and attract angel investors.

Many clubs were reluctant to share information on their activities for fear of receiving too many irrelevant proposals and business plans. Therefore, readers are cautioned to carefully evaluate the criteria for each club before sending any information. Every club listed has at least one limitation related to stage of development, line of business, location, or the amount of capital. Throughout, quoted information about a club is from that organization's brochure or from interviews with a club contact. This directory was compiled by Nancy Scarlato, who is an associate at my firm, Financial Communications Associates, Inc.

VENTURE CAPITAL CLUBS

A

ALABAMA
◆ **Birmingham Venture Club**
c/o Birmingham Chamber of Commerce
P.O. Box 10127
Birmingham, AL 35202
(205) 323-5461
CONTACT: Bill Sisson or Riva Rooker
ACTIVITIES: Started in 1985. Luncheon meetings are every other month; annual meeting in November. Club concentrates on Birm-

ingham region; only Alabama-based companies can participate. Annual dues are $90 plus $75 for each additional member of the same organization.

PRESENTATION OPPORTUNITIES: Attendees have the opportunity to introduce themselves and their business to the group.

ALASKA
See Private Capital Networks—AlaskaNet

ARIZONA
◆ **Arizona Venture Capital Conference**
Phoenix Chamber of Commerce
201 North Central Avenue, Suite 2700
Phoenix, AZ 85073
(602) 495-6488
FAX: (602) 495-8913
CONTACT: Amy Irwin

ACTIVITIES: Annual conference. Started in 1992. "Conference has infused more than $50 million into the state, and more than 36 percent of the presenting companies have received their desired investment." No restrictions as far as industry, although hi-tech and medicine are strongly represented. There is a $75 fee to apply. Companies selected to present pay an additional $175.

PRESENTATION OPPORTUNITIES: Ten to 12 new companies are selected to present. Each company is provided with a coaching team.

ARKANSAS
◆ **Venture Capital Investors, Inc.**
2323 First Commercial Building
400 West Capitol Avenue
Little Rock, AR 72201-3441
(501) 372-5900
FAX: (501) 372-8181
CONTACT: Mary Good

ACTIVITIES: New organization with about 25 investors.
PRESENTATION OPPORTUNITIES: To be determined.

C

CALIFORNIA
◆ **CalTech/MIT Enterprise Forum®**
Industrial Relations Center 1-90
Pasadena, CA 91125
(626) 395-4041
FAX: (626) 795-7174

CONTACT: Gaylord Nichols
ACTIVITIES & PRESENTATION OPPORTUNITIES: *See entry for MIT Enterprise Forum®, Inc. in Massachusetts.*

◆ Central Coast MIT Enterprise Forum, Inc.

Interlink Electronics
546 Flynn Road
Camarillo, CA 93012
(805) 484-8855
FAX: (805) 484-8989
E-MAIL: snbforum@mit.edu
CONTACT: Paul Meyer
ACTIVITIES & PRESENTATION OPPORTUNITIES: *See entry for MIT Enterprise Forum®, Inc. in Massachusetts.*

◆ Community Entrepreneurs Association

P. O. Box 9838
San Rafael, CA 94912
(415) 435-4461
CONTACT: Dr. Richard Crandall, Executive Director
ACTIVITIES: This organization functions as a general business support group. Networking events and meetings provide a forum for Bay Area angels, entrepreneurs, and service providers to come together.
PRESENTATION OPPORTUNITIES: Meeting attendees have the opportunity to introduce themselves and explain what they do and what they're looking for at each meeting.

◆ Los Angeles Venture Association (LAVA)

626 Santa Monica Boulevard, Suite 129
Santa Monica, CA 90401-1066
(310) 450-9544
FAX: (310) 395-0657
E-MAIL: LAVA4@aol.com
CONTACT: Christine Buteyn, Executive Director
ACTIVITIES: Holds monthly breakfast meetings with speakers. "LAVA encourages the formation and growth of entrepreneurial businesses by providing access to the financial, professional, and educational resources of the Southern California business community." Annual membership dues range from $125 to $300. Also hosts Annual Investment Capital Conference.
PRESENTATION OPPORTUNITIES: There are two, four-minute business-plan presentations at each breakfast.

◆ **MIT Enterprise Forum® of the Bay Area, Inc.**
> (408) 323-2255
> E-MAIL: julie@lynch.com
> INTERNET: www.vlab.org
> CONTACT: Julie Lynch-Chairman
> ACTIVITIES & PRESENTATION OPPORTUNITIES: *See entry for MIT Enterprise Forum®, Inc. in Massachusetts.*

◆ **MIT Enterprise Forum® of San Diego**
> Executive Outsourcing International
> Suite 101 - 16528 Calle Pulido
> San Diego, CA 92128
> (619) 236-9400
> FAX: (619) 236-8940
> E-MAIL: sndforum@mit.edu
> CONTACT: John Foley
> ACTIVITIES & PRESENTATION OPPORTUNITIES: *See entry for MIT Enterprise Forum®, Inc. in Massachusetts.*

◆ **Northern California Venture Forum**
> c/o International Capital Resources
> 388 Market Street, Suite 500
> San Francisco, CA 94111
> (415) 296-2519
> INTERNET: www.icrnet.com
> CONTACT: Gerald Benjamin
> ACTIVITIES: Two investment conferences a year in May and November. Investors are interested in "direct investment into early- and expansion-stage transactions primarily in the 'Golden State.'" Diverse range of industries. Twenty to 30 accredited investors attend each meeting.
> PRESENTATION OPPORTUNITIES: Ten prescreened companies make 20-minute presentations.

◆ **Orange Coast Venture Group**
> 23011 Moulton Parkway, Suite F-2
> Laguna Hills, CA 92653
> (714) 859-3646
> FAX: (714) 859-1707
> EMAIL: OCVG1@aol.com
> CONTACT: Renee Wagner, Director
> ACTIVITIES: Formed in 1985 in order "to bring together the people in Orange County who are interested in a new enterprise and the process of creating it." Nine monthly luncheons a year, plus annual, members-only breakfast and dinner. Speakers at each luncheon.

Cost is $300 for the year.

PRESENTATION OPPORTUNITIES: One-minute forum at each meeting where members can introduce themselves and describe their capital needs.

◆ San Diego Venture Group
750 B Street, Suite 2400
San Diego, CA 92101
(619) 272-1985
INTERNET: www.sdvgroup.org
FAX: (619) 231-8055
CONTACT: Erin Hall, Director

ACTIVITIES: Incorporated in 1987. Monthly breakfast meetings, with panel discussions or speakers. Cost to join ranges from annual fees of $250 for individuals to $650 for corporate memberships, or $40 per meeting. Networking opportunity at each meeting.

PRESENTATION OPPORTUNITIES: One-minute forum has recently been discontinued. In the future, however, an entire meeting may be devoted to presentations.

◆ The Springboard Program
CONNECT-UCSD, MS-0176F
La Jolla, CA 92093-0176
(619) 534-6114
FAX: (619) 552-0649
INTERNET: www.connect.org/connect
CONTACT: William Otterson, Director

ACTIVITIES: Started in 1993, the program assists early-stage, high-tech and biotechnology companies in the San Diego area with strategic issues. Entrepreneurs don't have to be a member of CONNECT to participate in the program.

PRESENTATION OPPORTUNITIES: Once a week (about 30 times a year) CONNECT convenes a panel of appropriate experts and capital providers. Companies make 10- to 15-minute presentations to a panel of up to 20 experts specifically selected for the companies making the presentations. Free to entrepreneurs. Annual technology financial forum. In February, 36 companies seeking funding are selected to present to an audience of investors during a two-day conference. Concept forum is held the night before the conference where an additional 15 early-stage companies set up product displays in a trade-show format. Annual biotechnology/medical technology partnership forum in November.

COLORADO

◆ **Rockies Venture Club**

190 East 9th Avenue, Suite 320
Denver, CO 80203
(303) 831-4174
FAX: (303) 832-4920
E-MAIL: maita@earthlink.net
INTERNET: www.metzger.com/rvc
CONTACT: Maita Lester

ACTIVITIES: Monthly dinner meetings featuring networking time, a speaker, one or two presentations by chief executives of emerging growth companies, and three or four presentations from entrepreneurs seeking capital. Membership is not restricted by state; however, most members live in Colorado. Annual membership fees start at $75 for individuals. The club also hosts an annual conference that provides a forum for issues important to the business and financial communities, and a fall financing forum that is a trade show of new financing sources.

PRESENTATION OPPORTUNITIES: Members can make a five-minute presentation at the monthly meetings, up to two times a year. Three to four companies present at each meeting.

◆ **Venture Capital in the Rockies**

KPMG Peat Marwick
707 17th Street, Suite 2300
Denver, CO 80202
(303) 296-2323
FAX: (303) 295-8819
CONTACT: Judy Whitten

ACTIVITIES: Annual conference sponsored jointly by KPMG Peat Marwick and Venture Capital Association of Colorado, an institutional, venture capital organization for start-up and early-stage companies seeking capital. Companies must be located in the Rocky Mountain states of Idaho, Montana, Utah, Nevada, Wyoming, Colorado, Arizona, or New Mexico. About 15 emerging growth companies are selected to present.

CONNECTICUT

◆ **Connecticut Venture Group**

425 Katona Drive
Fairfield, CT 06430
(203) 333-3284
FAX: (203) 367-3951
CONTACT: Mike Roer

ACTIVITIES: Founded in 1974, the group holds 23 networking luncheons a year among three chapters, located in Stamford, New Haven, and Hartford. Each luncheon has a speaker on topics of interest to entrepreneurs and/or an entrepreneurial case history. There is also an annual venture fair. Members include investment bankers, service providers, venture capitalists, and entrepreneurs. Annual membership fees range from $300 for individuals to $1,000 for corporations.

PRESENTATION OPPORTUNITIES: 25 ventures are selected to make presentations at the annual venture fair.

◆ **MIT Enterprise Forum® of Connecticut**
1 American Row
Hartford, CT 06103
(860) 251-5000
FAX: (860) 251-5199
E-MAIL: conforum@mit.edu
CONTACT: Frank Marco
ACTIVITIES & PRESENTATION OPPORTUNITIES: *See entry for MIT Enterprise Forum®, Inc. in Massachusetts.*

DELAWARE

◆ **Delaware Entrepreneurs' Forum**
P.O. Box 278
Yorklyn, DE 19736
(302) 652-4241
CONTACT: Christopher Klemm at (610) 648-0515
ACTIVITIES: Monthly programs with topics interesting to entrepreneurs. Venture fair once a year. Looking for companies with significant growth potential, range of industries, with investments from seed to $5 million. Concentrates on Delaware and surrounding areas. Monthly meetings are free, but there is a fee to present at the venture fair.

PRESENTATION OPPORTUNITIES: Twenty-four companies nominated by service providers and then selected by committee give eight-minute presentations at the venture fair. Coaching is provided.

FLORIDA

◆ **Central Florida Innovation Corporation**
12424 Research Parkway, Suite 350
Orlando, FL 32826
(407) 277-5411

FAX: (407) 277-2182
E-MAIL: cfic@cfic.org
CONTACT: Christa Santos

ACTIVITIES: Provides assistance to start-ups and emerging business-es within a two-hour drive of Orlando through its Innovation and Commercialization Center. The group also sponsors the Emerging Business Network (EBN), which is an alliance of business owners, investors, and service providers who meet monthly for networking purposes. There is also an annual venture capital conference for eco-nomic development and other professional service organizations.

PRESENTATION OPPORTUNITIES: Each monthly meeting offers a two-minute forum for entrepreneurs to introduce themselves and describe their capital needs. Once each quarter the EBN has Entre-preneur Night. Two or three companies are solicited to make 12-minute presentations. In addition, 12 to 14 companies are selected to make 12-minute presentations at the annual conference. Training and coaching support is provided.

◆ North Florida Venture Capital Network

7400 Bay Meadows Way-Suite 201
Jacksonville, FL 32256
(904) 730-4726
FAX: (904) 730-4711
CONTACT: Pamela Phillips

ACTIVITIES: Meets once a month to discuss investment opportuni-ties. Businesses must have a nexus to the north Florida area. Mainly interested in manufacturing companies. There is a $25 fee for appli-cation processing to present in front of the group. Annual member-ship dues are $195.

PRESENTATION OPPORTUNITIES: At least two companies present at every meeting for 15 minutes each. There is an annual two-day forum at which approximately 24 companies present to an audience of about 200 investors.

◆ Florida Venture Forum

Florida International University
2600 Douglas Road, Suite 311
Coral Gables, FL 33134
(305) 446-5060
FAX: (305) 443-4607
INTERNET: www.fiu.edu/~fvf
CONTACT: Jeanne Becker

ACTIVITIES: The forum meets approximately nine times a year and alternates between an educational presentation and a company pro-file. A committee selects Florida-based companies with high growth potential to present at these meetings. There is also an annual venture capital conference for companies based anywhere in the southeastern United States. The forum reports that the annual conference has raised more than $51 million over the last five years. Annual membership dues range from $200 to $500.

PRESENTATION OPPORTUNITIES: One company is selected every other month to make a 20-minute presentation at the forum. Approximately 20 companies are selected to make 12-minute presentations at the annual venture capital conference.

◆ **The Founders Forum**
Downtown Office Center
1900 South Harbor City Boulevard
Melbourne, FL 32901
(407) 984-1900
FAX: (407) 951-4227
CONTACT: Harry Brandon

ACTIVITIES: Established in 1985. Primarily a business incubator. However, nine meetings a year are held for networking purposes.
PRESENTATION OPPORTUNITIES: Attendees have the opportunity to introduce themselves/products/services at each meeting. Also three to five companies are selected to make three-minute presentations.

◆ **Gainesville Area Innovation Network**
Southern Technology Applications Center
P.O. Box 13442
Gainesville, FL 32604
(352) 466-4387
FAX: (352) 294-7802
E-MAIL: gain@asn.org
CONTACT: Carol Ann Dykes or Tina King

ACTIVITIES: Affiliated with the University of Florida. Formed in 1985 "to provide networking and educational opportunities to assist and encourage the entrepreneurial efforts of its members." Monthly luncheon meetings. Annual membership fees range from $20 to $100. Focus is primarily northern Florida companies in technology-based businesses. Business plans are reviewed and executive summaries are circulated.
PRESENTATION OPPORTUNITIES: Luncheon attendees can introduce themselves.

◆ **Gold Coast Venture Capital Club**
11401-A West Palmetto Park Road, Suite 202
Boca Raton, FL 3 3428
(561) 488-4505

FAX: (561) 487-4483

CONTACT: Greg Young

ACTIVITIES: Founded in 1984. Eleven monthly dinner meetings a year. Affiliated with Florida Atlantic University. Annual dues range from $100 for individuals to $150 for corporations. Mainly interested in south Florida companies.

PRESENTATION OPPORTUNITIES: Attendees can introduce themselves and their product/service. At the beginning of each regular meeting one company makes a 10-minute presentation. Companies must submit a complete business plan to a screening committee to be selected. Club holds a venture forum three times a year in which one company, selected by the executive committee, presents its business plan.

G

GEORGIA

◆ **Network for Business Acquisitions and Investments (NBA&I)**
3873 Roswell Road NW, Suite 4
Atlanta, GA 30342
(404) 261-2434
FAX: (404) 261-2434
CONTACT: Jerry Martin

ACTIVITIES: Started in 1995. Group's mission is to promote and facilitate business relationships for individuals and organizations interested in acquisitions, investments, and strategic alliances. The group, which meets monthly, has completed almost 20 deals totaling over $7.5 million. The smallest investment was $10,000; the largest was $3 million. No restrictions related to geography, industry, or size of deal; however, most companies are located in Atlanta or surrounding communities. Cost to join NBA&I varies for entrepreneurs, members, meeting guests, and sponsors.

PRESENTATION OPPORTUNITIES: Two to four entrepreneurs make 10- to 15-minute presentations at each meeting.

H

HAWAII

◆ **Hawaii Venture Capital Association**
805 Kainui Drive
Kailua, HI 96734-2025
PHONE: (808) 262-7329
FAX: (808) 263-4982
CONTACT: Joe Megna

ACTIVITIES: Started in 1988. Has a business plan review panel, monthly meetings, and educational conferences. Also has enterprise forum for emerging technology-based businesses and alternative-financing workshops. Cost is $100 for individuals and $200 for corporate memberships.

PRESENTATION OPPORTUNITIES: Entrepreneurs can give presentations to a panel of experts with audience participation. The audience consists of investors, venture capitalists, and service providers.

IDAHO

◆ Rocky Mountain Venture Group, c/o Department of Energy
2300 North Yellowstone
Idaho Falls, ID 83401
(208) 526-1181
FAX: (208) 529-2388
E-MAIL: blyth_rl@srb.net
CONTACT: Bob Blythe

ACTIVITIES: Monthly information and networking forums. Quarterly angel forums. Entrepreneurs restricted to eastern Idaho region. No restrictions on industry, but most companies are low-tech.

PRESENTATION OPPORTUNITIES: A screening committee selects three companies to make 15- to 20-minute presentations. Coaching and support are provided.

See also Colorado—Venture Capital in the Rockies

ILLINOIS

◆ MIT Enterprise Forum® of Chicago
8 South Michigan Avenue
Suite 1000
Chicago, IL 60603
(312) 782-4951
FAX: (312) 580-0165
E-MAIL: chiforum@mit.edu or mit@gss.net
CONTACT: Jerry Mitchell (630) 305-0005

ACTIVITIES & PRESENTATION OPPORTUNITIES: *See entry for MIT Enterprise Forum®, Inc. in Massachusetts.*

INDIANA

◆ Entrepreneurs' Alliance of Indiana
P.O. Box 90096
Indianapolis, IN 46240-0096
(317) 253-1244
FAX: (317) 253-1211
CONTACT: Margo Jaqua

ACTIVITIES: Monthly dinner meetings. The alliance's purpose is to "encourage and support the entrepreneurial spirit of Indiana businesses through an alliance of entrepreneurs helping entrepreneurs." Provides networking opportunities among members, who include investors, service providers, and entrepreneurs. Membership is $45 per year.

PRESENTATION OPPORTUNITIES: None.

◆ **Indiana Private Investor's Network (INPIN)**
216 West Allen Street
Bloomington, IN 47403
(812) 339-8937
FAX: (812) 335-7352
CONTACT: Seema Pawar

ACTIVITIES: Holds occasional luncheon meetings with presentations. There is no restriction as to industry, although businesses must be based in Indiana. There is a panel that reviews business plans and mails them to appropriate investors. INPIN is moving toward development of a computer-based system matching entrepreneurs and investors.

PRESENTATION OPPORTUNITIES: None.

◆ **Michiana Investment Network**
Small Business Development Center
300 North Michigan Street
South Bend, IN 46601
(219) 282-4350
FAX: (219) 236-1056
CONTACT: Carolyn Anderson

ACTIVITIES: Quarterly luncheon meetings that provide a forum for networking opportunities. Annual membership fee is $35.

PRESENTATION OPPORTUNITIES: A screening committee evaluates business plans and selects two or three companies to present at each meeting.

◆ **Venture Club of Indiana**
P.O. Box 40872
Indianapolis, IN 46240-0872
(317) 253-1244
FAX: (317) 253-1211
E-MAIL: mmjaqua@msn.com
CONTACT: Margo Jaqua

ACTIVITIES: Founded in 1984. The club holds monthly luncheon meetings with networking opportunities and speakers. Annual membership cost is $250, which includes cost of the luncheons, a newsletter, and a membership directory. Associate memberships for those outside of a 50-mile radius of Indianapolis are $50 per year.

PRESENTATION OPPORTUNITIES: Each meeting has two, five-minute presentations by entrepreneurs seeking capital.

IOWA

◆ Venture Network of Iowa

Iowa Department of Economic Development
200 East Grand St.
Des Moines, IA 50309
(515) 242-4874
FAX: (515) 242-4776
E-MAIL: brice.nelson@ided.state.ia.us
CONTACT: Brice Nelson

ACTIVITIES: Holds meetings every other month for the purpose of bringing together entrepreneurs and investors in Iowa. Also sponsors the Virtual Management Assistance Program (VMAP), a computer-based matching program for entrepreneurs, service providers, and, to a lesser extent, investors.

PRESENTATION OPPORTUNITIES: Each meeting has a two-minute forum in which up to five companies can introduce themselves and describe their funding needs.

KANSAS

◆ Kansas Technology Enterprise Corporation (KTEC)

1st Floor, 214 SW 6th Avenue
Topeka, KS 66603-3719
(785) 296-5272
FAX: (785) 296-1160
CONTACT: Rich Bendis

ACTIVITIES: KTEC sponsors two venture capital conferences a year in conjunction with Ernst & Young. Emphasis is on preseed, seed, and first-round venture capital for companies in Kansas and, to some extent, Missouri.

PRESENTATION OPPORTUNITIES: Up to 10 companies are selected to present at each conference. Other presentation opportunities exist on a case-by-case basis.

KENTUCKY

◆ Venture Club of Louisville

304 West Liberty, Suite 301
Louisville, KY 40202
(502) 589-6868

CONTACT: Rebecca Craig, Club Administrator, or Robert Ogden, President

ACTIVITIES: Started in 1995 for the purpose of "facilitating and encouraging the expansion of business and commercial investment activities in the region." Holds monthly luncheon meetings with networking opportunities and speakers. No restriction as to type of industry.

PRESENTATION OPPORTUNITIES: Before each meeting, three entrepreneurs are selected by committee to make five-minute presentations. Also, each meeting features any number of one-minute "announcements" or introductions.

L

LOUISIANA

◆ The Venture Network

601 Poydras St.-Suite 1700
New Orleans, LA 70130
(504) 527-6936
FAX: (504) 887-1344
CONTACT: Chris Laborde, Presiding Officer, or the Chamber—New Orleans and the River Region at (504) 527-6935 or (800) 949-7890.

ACTIVITIES: Organized in 1985 to provide a forum for entrepreneurs and investors. Holds breakfast meetings seven times a year, featuring speakers, educational seminars, and presentations from investors on entrepreneurship and access to capital. Fees are $25 per meeting.

PRESENTATION OPPORTUNITIES: Entrepreneurs can make presentations at most meetings with advance reservations.

M

MAINE

◆ Maine Investment Exchange (MIX)

Maine and Company
120 Exchange Street
Portland, ME 04101
(207) 871-0234
FAX: (207) 775-6716
E-MAIL: business@maineco.org
CONTACT: Gail Pfiefle

ACTIVITIES: Venture capital forums are scheduled on an as-needed basis. No restrictions as to location or industry. Cost is $50 to submit an application to present.

PRESENTATION OPPORTUNITIES: Arranged as necessary. Usually

hold forums every two months, with two or three entrepreneurs making 15-minute presentations.

MARYLAND

◆ **Baltimore-Washington Venture Group (B-WVG)**
Dingman Center for Entrepreneurship
The Robert H. Smith School of Business
4361 Van Munching Hall
The University of Maryland
College Park, MD 20742-1815
(301) 405-2144
FAX: (301) 314-9152
CONTACT: Angela Tandy

ACTIVITIES: B-WVG holds monthly breakfast meetings that are networking events with speakers on topics of interest to entrepreneurs. Membership is limited to those in the D.C. "Metroplex" area.

PRESENTATION OPPORTUNITIES: B-WVG is mostly responsible for selecting entrepreneurs to present to members of Private Investor Network (PIN), listed below. It does not have its own presentation opportunities.

◆ **Private Investors' Network (PIN)**

402 Maple Ave. West
Vienna, VA 22180
(703) 255-4930
FAX: (703) 255-4931
CONTACT: John May

ACTIVITIES: PIN meets once a month, 10 times a year. Investments range from $250,000 to $3 million. Companies must be located in Maryland, Virginia, or Washington, D.C. Cost for entrepreneurs is $150 for business plan review and additional $150 if selected to present at a PIN meeting. PIN also provides to its investor-members a monthly "circulation of opportunities" that is a two-page briefing provided on each company seeking investments.

PRESENTATION OPPORTUNITIES: Three or four companies present for 10 minutes, followed by a five-minute question-and-answer session. Coaching is provided.

MASSACHUSETTS

◆ **MIT Enterprise Forum®, Inc.**
28 Carleton St.
Building E32-330
Cambridge, MA 02139
(617) 253-0015
FAX: (617) 258-0532

CONTACT: Edmund Dunn, Director

ACTIVITIES: The MIT Enterprise Forum®, Inc. was founded in 1978; today it has 14 chapters located throughout the country and four international chapters. Its mission is to promote the formation and growth of technologically oriented companies through a series of educational programs. All chapters share this mission, although the execution of the program varies. Some activities of the forum include entrepreneurial educational programs, professional seminars, start-up clinics, and business-plan workshops.

PRESENTATION OPPORTUNITIES: Available from time to time, in the form of case studies of actual business plans.

◆ MIT Enterprise Forum® of Cambridge

28 Carleton St.
Building E32-330
Cambridge, MA 02139
(617) 253-8240
FAX: (617) 258-0532
E-MAIL: mitefcmb@mit.edu
INTERNET: http://www.mitforum-cambridge.org
CONTACT: Jack Derby at (617) 266-9266

ACTIVITIES & PRESENTATION OPPORTUNITIES: *See MIT Enterprise Forum®, Inc. listing above.*

◆ 128 Venture Capital Group

Bedford Road
Lincoln, MA 01773
PHONE/FAX: (781) 259-8776
CONTACT: Michael Belanger, President

ACTIVITIES: Formed in 1983. To date it has had 181 consecutive meetings. Its purpose is to provide a venue "for private investors seeking early contact with emerging business ventures." Monthly meetings cost between $35 and $45; 80 to 90 people including entrepreneurs, capital providers, service providers, and management attend.

PRESENTATION OPPORTUNITIES: Attendees can briefly introduce themselves and outline their needs/services at each meeting.

◆ Technology Capital Network (TCN) at MIT

P.O. Box 425936
Cambridge, MA 02142
CONTACT: Bard Salmon at (617) 253-7163 or
Betty Kadis (617) 253-8214
FAX: (617) 258-7395

ACTIVITIES: TCN sponsors venture capital forums three times a year (typically February, May, and October). Capital-pooling meetings are sponsored approximately every other month. Also sponsors entrepreneurs' financing roundtables 10 times a year. These breakfast meetings are limited to entrepreneurs. TCN is also a computer-based matching service. (*For a full description, see the Private Capital Networks section.*)

PRESENTATION OPPORTUNITIES: Up to 10 Massachusetts-based companies present to investors at the venture capital forums. Each capital-pooling meeting has four companies that already have some financing present to an audience of investors, with the goal of attracting additional funding.

◆ Venture-Preneurs™ Network
85 East India Row, Suite 23B
Boston, MA 02110
(617) 720-1535
FAX: (617) 720-1525
E-MAIL: vpn@tiac.net
INTERNET: www.venturepreneurs.com
CONTACT: Michael Gordon

ACTIVITIES: Breakfast meetings held two to three times a year at which entrepreneurs, capital providers, service providers, and management candidates come together to pursue their business interests. Venture-Preneurs also holds workshops on financing, provides management consulting, and has an angel fund, which is a syndicate of investors focusing on investments in early-stage-technology companies. There are also two to three "member-only" events each year. Annual membership is $195, or $45 per meeting.

PRESENTATION OPPORTUNITIES: Four to six entrepreneurs present their business plans at each breakfast meeting.

MICHIGAN
◆ Southeastern Michigan Venture Group
20630 Harper Avenue, Suite 103
Harper Woods, MI 48225
(313) 886-2331
CONTACT: Carl Meyering, Chairman or George Richmond, President

ACTIVITIES: Organized in 1983 to provide a forum for entrepreneurs to meet investors and service providers. The group has made $48 million in investments since its inception. Holds networking meetings monthly, 10 months a year. Entrepreneurs required to submit a business plan summary in advance; there are some selective criteria related to type of business. No geographic restriction. There is a $25 charge to attend each meeting.

PRESENTATION OPPORTUNITIES: Entrepreneurs can make a one-minute presentation.

◆ Traverse Bay Enterprise Forum

P.O. Box 506
Traverse City, MI 49685-0506
(616) 929-5017
FAX: (616) 929-5012
E-MAIL: dbeldin@nwm.cog.mi.us
CONTACT: Richard Beldin

ACTIVITIES: Quarterly forums for the purpose of bringing together entrepreneurs and investors in the lower-northwest Michigan area.
PRESENTATION OPPORTUNITIES: Four to five formal, 10-minute presentations are made at each forum. In addition, forum attendees can make three-minute presentations.

◆ Venture Center, Inc.

P.O. Box 27186
Lansing, MI 48909-7186
(517) 337-2670
FAX: (517) 337-2672
E-MAIL: shawbr@pilot.msu.edu
INTERNET: www.bus.msu.edu/venture/
CONTACT: Brad Shaw

ACTIVITIES: The center works with entrepreneurs to promote them to investors. It operates out of Michigan State University and in conjunction with the mid-Michigan Advisory Council. It primarily serves the Mid-Michigan area; there are no restrictions as to industry.
PRESENTATION OPPORTUNITIES: Available through the Mid-Michigan Advisory Council.

MINNESOTA

◆ The Collaborative

10 South Fifth Street, Suite 415
Minneapolis, MN 55402-1004
(612) 338-3828
FAX: (612) 338-1876
CONTACT: Beth Dunham

ACTIVITIES: Holds 10 monthly networking meetings a year and approximately 15 workshops of interest to entrepreneurs. In addition, the Collaborative holds two all-day venture finance conferences in the fall and spring. Members are located primarily throughout Minnesota; however, some are from Wisconsin, North Dakota, and South Dakota. There is no restriction as to industry. Annual membership fees range from $395 at the entrepreneurial level to $795 at the professional level.

PRESENTATION OPPORTUNITIES: Fifteen companies are selected to make 12-minute presentations at the venture finance conferences. Thirty to 40 additional companies can showcase business plans and products at the conference.

MISSISSIPPI

See Ace-Net, described in Chapter 2: Securing Capital from Angels
See also National Private Capital Networks

MISSOURI

◆ Missouri Venture Forum

917 Locust Street, 5th Floor
St. Louis, MO 63101
(314) 241-2683
FAX: (314) 621-2529
CONTACT: Judy Taylor

ACTIVITIES: The forum is 13 years old and holds breakfast networking meetings ten times a year. Companies are mostly from St. Louis. Annual membership cost is $295; $25 to sit in on a meeting as a guest. Reservations required.

PRESENTATION OPPORTUNITIES: Entrepreneurs can apply to present at a meeting.

MONTANA

See Private Capital Networks—Montana Private Capital Network
See also Colorado—Venture Capital in the Rockies and see Ace-Net , described in Chapter 2: Securing Capital from Angels.

N

NEBRASKA

◆ Nebraska Center for Entrepreneurship

CBA 209
University of Nebraska
Lincoln, NE 68588-0487
(402) 472-3353
CONTACT: Dr. Terry Sebora

ACTIVITIES: Frequently holds seminars and workshops on topics such as business plan preparation and venture capital. Networking functions are sponsored quarterly. There is also an annual conference with networking opportunities and speakers on educational topics. Would consider having a venture fair if there is enough interest.

PRESENTATION OPPORTUNITIES: Informal and on an as-needed basis.

NEVADA

See Colorado—Venture Capital in the Rockies
See also Ace-Net, described in Chapter 2: Securing Capital from Angels.
See also Private Capital Network

NEW HAMPSHIRE

◆ **Nashua Breakfast Club**
  c/o R. Morley, Inc.
  586 Nashua Street, Suite 56
  Milford, NH 03055
  (603) 878-4365
  CONTACT: Dick Morley

ACTIVITIES: Breakfast meeting once a month. Restricted to high-tech businesses within one hour's traveling time of southern New Hampshire. Businesses must need preseed capital.

PRESENTATION OPPORTUNITIES: Send business plans, and the club will notify the entrepreneur if there is interest to meet further.

NEW JERSEY

◆ **Venture Association of New Jersey**
  P.O. Box 1982
  Morristown, NJ 07962-1982
  (973) 267-4200
  FAX: (973) 984-9634
  E-MAIL: 76044.105@compuserve.com
  INTERNET: www.vanj.com
  CONTACT: Jay Trien

ACTIVITIES: Monthly meetings 11 times a year to stimulate interaction between businesses and investors. Membership dues range from $895 (for sponsorship), to $400 (includes luncheons), to $125 (for membership only).

PRESENTATION OPPORTUNITIES: Three companies are chosen each month to make five-minute presentations in front of the group.

NEW MEXICO

See Colorado—Venture Capital in the Rockies
See also Ace-Net, described in Chapter 2: Securing Capital from Angels.
See also Private Capital Network

◆ **Western New York Venture Association (WNYVA)**

Baird Research Park
1576 Sweet Home Road
Amherst, NY 14228
(716) 636-3626
FAX: (716) 636-3630
CONTACT: John A. McGowan

ACTIVITIES: Founded in 1989, the association holds quarterly net-working events. Most members are located in the Buffalo area. Membership fees are $45 per year for individuals, and $250 for corporate sponsors.

PRESENTATION OPPORTUNITIES: WNYVA actively solicits business plans in order to select two companies to present at each meeting. Coaching and support are provided.

◆ **Long Island Venture Group**

Business Development Center
Room 217
145 Hofstra University
Hempstead, NY 11549-1450
(516) 463-6326
FAX: (516) 463-3907
CONTACT: Bridget Del Gaudio

ACTIVITIES: Monthly breakfast meetings are structured to encourage networking and deal making. Periodically, there are special events, such as business planning clinics and seminars. Annual membership dues are $250.

PRESENTATION OPPORTUNITIES: There is a one-minute forum at each meeting at which attendees can introduce their business/service to the group.

◆ **MIT Enterprise Forum® of New York City, Inc.**

420 Lexington Avenue, Room 2400
New York, NY 10170
(212) 681-1112
FAX: (212) 286-9026
E-MAIL: nycforum@mit.edu
CONTACT: Brian Finkel (212) 845-7150

ACTIVITIES & PRESENTATION OPPORTUNITIES: *See entry for MIT Enterprise Forum®, Inc., in Massachusetts.*

◆ **The New York Angel Investors Program**

New York New Media Association
55 Broad Street

New York, NY 10004
(212) 785-7898
FAX: (212) 785-7963
E-MAIL: angels@nynma.org
INTERNET: www.nynma.org/programs/
CONTACT: Brian Horey

ACTIVITIES: Monthly meetings bring together investors and companies in the new-media industry seeking between $100,000 and $1,000,000 in capital. *Investments are restricted to new-media businesses.*

PRESENTATION OPPORTUNITIES: Two companies present at each meeting.

NORTH CAROLINA

◆ **Council for Entrepreneurial Development (CED)**
104 Alexander Drive
P.O. Box 13353
Research Triangle Park, NC 27709-3353
(919) 549-7500
FAX: (919) 549-7405
CONTACT: Monica Doss

ACTIVITIES: CED has a variety of programs geared toward assisting entrepreneurs. There are monthly programs, special-interest round tables, training seminars, and several networking opportunities. There are also four conferences a year, one of which focuses on venture capital. CED concentrates on assisting companies in many different industries that are located in North Carolina. CED is the hub for seven other entrepreneurial councils located throughout the state.

PRESENTATION OPPORTUNITIES: Companies are selected by a screening committee to present at each of the conferences. Up to 15 entrepreneurs present at the venture conference.

NORTH DAKOTA

◆ **North Dakota Development Fund**
1833 East Bismarck Expressway
Bismarck, ND 58504-6708
(701) 328-5310
FAX: (701) 328-5320
CONTACT: Bryan Dvirnak

ACTIVITIES: Started in 1991. The fund manages $25 million. Investment is usually between $100,000 and $300,000 in new or expanding businesses in or relocating to North Dakota. Primary industries are manufacturing and high-tech. Will not consider agriculture.

PRESENTATION OPPORTUNITIES: On a case-by-case basis.

OHIO

◆ **Greater Cincinnati Venture Association (GCVA)**
Greater Cincinnati Chamber of Commerce
441 Vine Street
300 Carew Tower
Cincinnati, OH 45202-2812
(513) 579-3128
FAX: (513) 579-3101
E-MAIL: rganim@gccc.com
CONTACT: Rachel Ganim

ACTIVITIES: Meets monthly nine times a year for presentations and networking opportunities. Annual memberships are $275 for corporations and $110 for individuals. Recently, several members of the GCVA formed a $200,000 venture capital fund—Cincinnati Venture One Ltd. There are no restrictions on type of industry, however, but the business must provide a benefit to the greater Cincinnati area.

PRESENTATION OPPORTUNITIES: Each meeting has two or three presentations by entrepreneurs.

◆ **Ohio Venture Association (OVA)**
1127 Euclid Avenue, Suite 343
Cleveland, OH 44115
(216) 566-8884
FAX: (216) 696-2582
CONTACT: Ron Cohen

ACTIVITIES: OVA meets monthly for lunch. There are networking opportunities and a speaker on topics of interest to entrepreneurs. Through the "Hatch-an-Egg" mentoring program, entrepreneurs may receive up to two hours of free consultation from other OVA members on topics of concern. Membership fees are $120 for individuals and $300 for corporations.

PRESENTATION OPPORTUNITIES: Each meeting has a five-minute forum at which two or three entrepreneurs make presentations to the group.

OKLAHOMA

◆ **Entrepreneurs of Tulsa**
401 South Boston
Mid-Continent Tower, 18th Floor, Suite 1810
Tulsa, OK 74103-4018
(918) 582-6131
FAX: (918) 584-4213

CONTACT: Margot Arnold

ACTIVITIES: Holds monthly educational and networking meetings. Focus is on providing support to new businesses in the northeastern Oklahoma area.

PRESENTATION OPPORTUNITIES: Occasionally, on an as-needed basis.

OREGON

◆ **Oregon Enterprise Forum**

2611 SW Third Avenue, Suite 200
Portland, OR 97201
(503) 222-2270
FAX: (503) 241-0827
E-MAIL: info@oef.org
INTERNET: www.oef.org
CONTACT: Jim Berchtold

ACTIVITIES & PRESENTATION OPPORTUNITIES: *See entry for MIT Enterprise Forum®, Inc. in Massachusetts.*

P

PENNSYLVANIA

◆ **Greater Philadelphia Venture Group**

200 South Broad Street, Suite 700
Philadelphia, PA 19102-3896
(215) 790-3689
FAX: (215) 790-3601
E-MAIL: ckeim@gpcc.com
INTERNET: www.gpcc.com
CONTACT: Carolyn Keim

ACTIVITIES: A council of the Greater Philadelphia Chamber of Commerce. Formerly known as the Delaware Valley Venture Group. Monthly networking events held from September through June. Cosponsor of the Mid-Atlantic Venture Fair. Annual memberships range from $150 for individuals to $1,500 to $2,000 for corporations.

PRESENTATION OPPORTUNITIES: None at monthly events. Entrepreneurs may apply to be selected to present at the Mid-Atlantic Venture Fair.

◆ **Loosely Organized Retired Executives (LORE)**

c/o Verus Corporation
5 Radnor Corporate Center
100 Matsonford Road, Suite 520
Radnor, PA 19087
(610) 964-8452

FAX: (610) 964-3630

CONTACT: J. Tolson

ACTIVITIES: None.

PRESENTATION OPPORTUNITIES: Will meet with companies by appointment after review of business plan. Companies must be located within a three-hour driving radius of metropolitan Philadelphia. Any industry acceptable. Interested primarily in companies with revenues.

◆ **MIT Enterprise Forum® of Pittsburgh, Inc.**
c/o Berthold Systems, Inc.
101 Corporation Drive
Aliquippa, PA 15001-4863
(724) 378-1900
FAX: (724) 378-1926
CONTACT: Bud Smith

ACTIVITIES & PRESENTATION OPPORTUNITIES: *See entry for MIT Enterprise Forum®, Inc. in Massachusetts.*

◆ **Pennsylvania Private Investors Group**
3625 Market Street, Suite 200
Philadelphia, PA 19104
(800) 288-3302
FAX: (215) 898-1063
CONTACT: Jeff Carpenter

ACTIVITIES: Monthly membership meeting provides a forum for entrepreneurs to present their business plans to investors to obtain financing. Companies must, among other criteria, be located within a 150-mile radius of Philadelphia and seeking between $25,000 and $5,000,000.

PRESENTATION OPPORTUNITIES: Two to three companies present at each meeting after being selected by a screening committee. The presentation is followed by a question-and-answer session.

R

RHODE ISLAND
◆ **Brown University Venture Forum**
P.O. Box 1949
Providence, RI 02912
(401) 863-3528
CONTACT: Joann Tillman

ACTIVITIES: Monthly meetings, sometimes with speakers or panel discussions. Also sponsors start-up clinics. Not limited in terms of industry or geography, although the forum is mainly interested in growth industries.

PRESENTATION OPPORTUNITIES: 15-minute presentations at select meetings by companies seeking capital. Business plans are used to review companies before they are selected by the committee to present.

◆ Hope Investors

2 Charles Street
Providence, RI 02904
(401) 861-0320
FAX: (401) 274-8942
CONTACT: Jim Twaddell

ACTIVITIES: Quarterly meetings. Interested primarily in technology, communications, and medical businesses located primarily in New England. Investments range from $500,000 to $3 million. Will accept business plans and respond only if the group is interested.

PRESENTATION OPPORTUNITIES: Only if there is interest within the group.

S

SOUTH CAROLINA

◆ Dare to Deal-Southeast Capital Connection

Center for Entrepreneurship, College of Charleston
66 George Street
Charleston, SC 29424-0001
(803) 953-5628
FAX: (803) 577-3480
CONTACT: Marcia Snyder

ACTIVITIES: Annual venture capital conference for companies located in South Carolina and the southeastern states.

PRESENTATION OPPORTUNITIES: A screening committee selects companies to present at the conference.

See also Private Capital Networks—Private Investor Network.

SOUTH DAKOTA

◆ Dakota Ventures

P.O. Box 8194
Rapid City, SD 57709
(605) 348-8441
CONTACT: Don Frankenfield

ACTIVITIES: Invests exclusively in South Dakota businesses, generally $100,000 to $200,000 range. Preferences are for general manufacturing and processing, high-tech, and agricultural, value-added businesses. Will not invest in restaurants, bars, or retailing concerns.

PRESENTATION OPPORTUNITIES: On a case-by-case basis.

TENNESSEE

See Private Capital Networks—Seed Capital Network. See also Ace-Net, described in Chapter 2: Securing Capital from Angels.

TEXAS

◆ MIT Enterprise Forum® of Dallas–Fort Worth, Inc.

Interactive Creations
1701 West Northwest Highway, Suite 220
Grapevine, TX 76051
(817) 424-5638
FAX: (817) 251-2228
E-MAIL: dalforum@mit.edu
CONTACT: Joseph Mannes at (817) 424-5638

ACTIVITIES & PRESENTATION OPPORTUNITIES: *See entry for MIT Enterprise Forum®, Inc. in Massachusetts.*

◆ MIT Enterprise Forum® of Texas, Inc.

711 Louisiana St., Suite 2900
Houston, TX 77002-2781
(713) 221-1303
FAX: (713) 221-1212
E-MAIL: houforum@mit.edu
CONTACT: Thomas Manford at (713) 221-1303

ACTIVITIES & PRESENTATION OPPORTUNITIES: *See entry for MIT Enterprise Forum®, Inc. in Massachusetts.*

241

UTAH

◆ Utah Venture Capital Conference

Wayne Brown Institute
P.O. Box 2135
Salt Lake City, UT 84110-2135
(801) 595-1141
FAX: (801) 595-1181
CONTACT: Lynn Butterfield

ACTIVITIES: Annual venture capital conference. Most companies are based in Utah; however, the conference is open to anyone. No restrictions as to industry, although most companies are technology-based.

PRESENTATION OPPORTUNITIES: On average, 12 to 14 companies present at each conference.

VERMONT

♦ **Vermont Investor's Forum**

c/o Green Mountain Capital
RD 1, Box 1503
Waterbury, VT 05676
(802) 244-8981
FAX: (802) 244-8990
CONTACT: Michael Sweatman

ACTIVITIES: Annual venture capital conference. Focus is on Vermont businesses, almost any industry. Tend towards early-stage companies requesting investments from $100,000 to $1 million.

PRESENTATION OPPORTUNITIES: About 10 companies are selected to make a formal presentation at each conference. Cost is $150.

VIRGINIA

♦ **Hampton Roads Private Investor Network**

Small Business Development Center (SBDC)
   of Hampton Roads, Inc.
400 Bank Street
Norfolk, VA 23501
(757) 825-2957
FAX: (757) 825-2960
E-MAIL: dfarley@hrccva.com
CONTACT: Debra Farley

ACTIVITIES: The SBDC, in addition to seminars, training programs, and workshops, has a relatively new computer-based matching network for entrepreneurs and investors. The one-year trial period has yielded nine deals ranging from $1,000 to $2.5 million. Entrepreneurs are selected to be promoted via this network based on evaluations from the SBDC. Entrepreneurs and investors are both located in the Hampton Roads Metropolitan Statistical Area; future plans include expansion to the Richmond and Charlottesville areas. There is no restriction as to industry.

PRESENTATION OPPORTUNITIES: None.

♦ **MIT Enterprise Forum® of Washington-Baltimore, Inc.**

P.O. Box 26203
Arlington, VA 22215
(703) 365-9023
FAX: (703) 521-2955
E-MAIL: dcbforum@mit.edu
CONTACT: John Franson

ACTIVITIES & PRESENTATION OPPORTUNITIES: *See entry for MIT Enterprise Forum®, Inc. in Massachusetts.*

◆ **Richmond Venture Capital Club**
 1407 Huguenot Road
 Midlothian, VA 23113
 (804) 794-1117
 CONTACT: Kathy Bradley
ACTIVITIES: Bimonthly meetings with speakers and networking opportunities. Focus is on the Richmond area and surrounding communities.
PRESENTATION OPPORTUNITIES: Board of directors selects up to five companies to make presentations at each meeting. Anyone can make a 30-second pitch during the introduction period.

W

WASHINGTON
◆ **Northwest Venture Group**
 P.O. Box 21693
 Seattle, WA 98111-3693
 (425) 746-1973
 CONTACT: Jim Goebelbecker, President

ACTIVITIES: Holds monthly breakfast meetings for networking. The group is interested in a wide variety of industries and companies that have significant growth potential on a local, national, or worldwide basis.
PRESENTATION OPPORTUNITIES: At monthly breakfast meetings up to three companies present to attendees for five minutes. Venture Advisory Panels (VAPs) allow companies to present to a panel of experts to solicit reactions. After a company has presented to a VAP and a five-minute forum, it may be selected to present to private investors who have expressed an interest in small, growing Northwest companies.

◆ **MIT Enterprise Forum® of the Northwest, Inc.**
 1319 Decker Ave. N., # 370
 Seattle, WA 98109
 (206) 283-9595
 FAX: (206) 283-9444
 INTERNET: www.mitwa.org/
 CONTACT: Michael Schwartz
ACTIVITIES & PRESENTATION OPPORTUNITIES: *See entry for MIT Enterprise Forum®, Inc. in Massachusetts.*

WEST VIRGINIA

See Ace-Net, described in Chapter 2. See also Private Capital Networks.

WISCONSIN

◆ **Wisconsin Venture Network**
P.O. Box 92093
Milwaukee, WI 53202
(414) 224-5988
FAX: (414) 271-4016
CONTACT: Paul Sweeney

ACTIVITIES: The network sponsors monthly luncheons with networking opportunities and also holds educational programs.
PRESENTATION OPPORTUNITIES: There are business plan presentations at each luncheon.

◆ **Wisconsin Innovation Network (WIN) Foundation**
P.O. Box 71
Madison, WI 53701-0071
(608) 256-8348
FAX: (608) 256-0333
CONTACT: Ken Syke

ACTIVITIES: Primarily an organization that devotes itself to supporting and encouraging entrepreneurs, WIN also sponsors an annual venture fair.
PRESENTATION OPPORTUNITIES: Ten to 15 high-growth, Wisconsin companies are selected to present at the venture fair.

WYOMING

See Colorado—Venture Capital in the Rockies
See Ace-Net, described in Chapter 2: Securing Capital from Angels.
See also Private Capital Networks

PRIVATE CAPITAL NETWORKS

UNLIKE VENTURE CAPITAL CLUBS, WHICH SPONSOR AND CREATE direct interaction between entrepreneurs and investors, private capital networks are primarily computer-based matching services. Specifically, private capital networks match entrepreneurs and investors by sorting on key variables such as deal size, location, line of business, and type of financing required. With the Internet emerging as a communications medium, private capital networks are emerging rapidly, with far-reaching implications for investors and entrepreneurs.

NATIONAL NETWORKS

◆ The Capital Network (TCN), Inc.

3925 West Braker Lane, Suite 406
Austin, TX 78759-5321
(512) 305-0826
FAX: (512) 305-0836
CONTACT: David Gerhardt
GEOGRAPHY: National

Started in 1989. Investments range from about $25,000 to $1 million, with an estimated $70 million invested in the past five years. The breakdown of ventures seeking capital is as follows: 28 percent, start-ups; 65 percent, between 1 and 5 years old; 7 percent, 5 years or older. The cost is $450 for entrepreneurs (6 months), $450 for private investors (one year), and $950 for institutional investors (one year).

◆ Environmental Capital Network (ECN)

416 Longshore Drive
Ann Arbor, MI 48105
(313) 996-8387
FAX: (734) 996-8732
EMAIL: kraab@recycle.com
INTERNET: http://bizserve.com/ecn/
CONTACT: Keith Raab
GEOGRAPHY: National

ECN provides company profiles of recycling and other environmental firms to investors nationwide. There are more than eighty individual, corporate, and professional investors on the network. The cost for companies that register with the network is $350 per year. Investors are charged $250 to $350.

◆ Investor's Circle

3220 Sacramento Street, Suite 21
San Francisco, CA 94115-2007
(415) 929-4910
FAX: (415) 929-4915
E-MAIL: icircle@aol.com
CONTACT: Cheri Arnold, Executive Director
GEOGRAPHY: National

The Investor's Circle operates a network that promotes investments in socially responsible ventures. Areas of interest include community development, health, international development, women and minority-led business, consumer products, education, energy, environment, and recycling. Company profiles are circulated to more than 150 investors on the network. Companies pay $300 for this service. Investors pay $1,000 to $1,500 a year.

◆ **Pacific Venture Capital Network (PACNET)**
   4199 Campus Drive, Suite 240
   Irvine, CA 92701
   (714) 509-2990
   FAX: (714) 509-2997
   CONTACT: Greg Collia
   GEOGRAPHY: National

Computerized matching program. Investors submit investment-interest profiles describing their investment criteria; entrepreneurs submit investment-opportunity profiles. Investors receive profiles that match their criteria. The cost for this service is $200 for entrepreneurs for six months, $200 for individual investors for one year, and $500 for institutional investors for one year. No geographic or industry restrictions. Investment dollar amounts range from under $10,000 to more than $1 million.

◆ **Private Capital Clearinghouse (PriCap)**
   45 Lyme Road
   Hanover, NH 03755
   (603) 643-7770
   www.pricap.com
   CONTACT: Paul Tierney
   GEOGRAPHY: National

PriCap is an Internet-based matching service for private investors and entrepreneurs who are seeking to complete private equity deals. The service allows investors and companies alike to screen potential partners based on geography, industry, and other criteria. Entrepreneurs using PriCap are typically looking for financing in the range of $250,000 to $5 million. PriCap works on a subscription basis. Minimum membership for a company is $150 for one year; for investors, $200 for six months.

◆ **Seed Capital Network**
   Suite 12
   8905 Kingston Pike
   Knoxville, TN 37923
   (423) 573-4655
   FAX: (423) 577-9989
   CONTACT: Robert Gaston
   GEOGRAPHY: National

Computer-based screening service that makes confidential linkups between investors and entrepreneurs. The average equity investment is $400,000. Investments range from $5,000 to $1.5 million. One-time charge to entrepreneurs is $260. Service is free to investors.

◆ Technology Capital Network (TCN) at MIT

P.O. Box 425936
Cambridge, MA 02142
(617) 253-7163
FAX: (617) 258-7395
CONTACT: Bard Salmon (617) 253-7163 or
Betty Kadis (617) 253-8214
GEOGRAPHY: National

Confidential, computerized matching service (called TecNet®) in operation since 1984. The network reports representing over $40 million in funds. In 1994, TCN activities resulted in $6.5 million being invested in 20 companies. Cost is $300 per year for entrepreneurs, $350 for individual investors, $700 for professional investors. There are no geographic or industry restrictions to participate in the network. TCN also sponsors venture capital forums, capital pooling meetings, and the entrepreneurs' financing roundtable (*See the Private Equity Capital Directory section for a description of these.*)

◆ U.S. Investor Network

P.O. Box 20161
Raleigh, NC 27619-0161
(919) 783-0614
FAX: (919) 833-8007
INTERNET: www.usinvestor.com
CONTACT: Pete Bechtel
GEOGRAPHY: International

Computer-based matching service that channels entrepreneurs to investors and alternate sources of financing. There are no industry restrictions. Investments range from $25,000 to $2 million. The service costs $8 per month for entrepreneurs, and $95 for six months for investors.

GEOGRAPHICALLY FOCUSED NETWORKS

◆ AlaskaNet

Juneau Economic Development Council
612 W. Willoughby Avenue
Suite A
Juneau, AK 99801-1724
(907) 463-3662
FAX: (907) 463-3929
INTERNET: www.ptialaska.net/~jedc/
CONTACT: Charles Northrip, Director or Pete McDowell
GEOGRAPHY: Alaska

Limited to entrepreneurial ventures in Alaska. Cost for both entrepreneurs (each year) and investors (one time) is $100. Matching process is manual.

◆ **Capital Resource Network**
> 4747 Troost Avenue
> Kansas City, MO 64110
> (816) 478-3777
> FAX: (816) 756-1530
> CONTACT: Hazel Mauro
> GEOGRAPHY: Kansas and Missouri

Most investors on this network are interested in manufacturing, biotechnology, and computer technology; however, there is no restriction on industry. Investments range from $25,000 to $500,000. Cost for both entrepreneurs and investors is $250.

◆ **Colorado Capital Alliance (CCA)**
> P.O. Box 19169
> Boulder, CO 80308-2169
> (303) 499-9646
> FAX: (303) 494-4146
> CONTACT: Marcia Shirmer or Gale Dunlap
> GEOGRAPHY: Colorado

CCA manages a confidential database of angels and entrepreneurs. Based on investor preferences, CCA delivers entrepreneurs' business summaries to investors while maintaining the entrepreneurs' anonymity. Most entrepreneurs are seeking between $50,000 and $1,000,000 in financing. Cost to entrepreneurs for one year's participation on the network is $200. The service is free to investors.

◆ **Kentucky Investment Capital Network (ICN)**
> 67 Wilkinson Boulevard
> Frankfort, KY 40601
> (800) 626-2930 or (502) 564-7140
> FAX: (502) 564-9758
> CONTACT: Norris Christian
> GEOGRAPHY: Kentucky

Computer-based matching program started in 1992. Managed by the Small Business Division of the Kentucky Cabinet for Economic Development. Businesses must be based in Kentucky, however investors can be from anywhere. Investments start at about $10,000. Most investors are interested in manufacturing industries. There is no charge for this service. ICN estimates that over 600 matches have been made since 1992.

◆ Montana Private Capital Network

P.O. Box 437
Poulson, MT 59860
(406) 883-5470
FAX: (406) 883-3050
E-MAIL: mpcnjan@marsweb.com
CONTACT: Jon Marchi
GEOGRAPHY: Montana

Computerized matching network sponsored by the state of Montana and private investors. Fee to entrepreneurs is $100 for one year. Investors are charged $200 for a two-year membership. There are no restrictions as to industry. However, recent matches have been made in the agriculture, timber, tourism, medical/health care, high-tech manufacturing, and service industries. Investments range between $100,000 and $1,000,000.

◆ North Carolina Investor Network (NCIN)

P.O. Box 20161
Raleigh, NC 27619-0161
(919) 783-0614
FAX: (919) 833-8007
CONTACT: Pete Bechtel
GEOGRAPHY: North Carolina

Multimedia matching service which uses the Internet and CD-ROMs to bring entrepreneurs and investors together. Entrepreneurs must first complete NCIN's training course, which prepares them to tackle the challenges of obtaining financing. There is no restriction as to industry. Investments range from $25,000 to $2 million; however, most companies are seeking around $1 million. Companies must also complete a Regulation D filing with the Securities and Exchange Commission (SEC) before subscribing to the system.

◆ Private Investor Network (PIN)

O'Connell Center for Entrepreneurship and Technology
University of South Carolina, Aiken
471 University Parkway
Aiken, SC 29801
(803) 641-3518
FAX: (803) 641-3362
CONTACT: Jeana Buckley
GEOGRAPHY: South Carolina

PIN is a confidential, computer-based matching service that brings together entrepreneurs and investors located in South Carolina. There are no restrictions as to type of business. PIN is a subscription-based service; fees to entrepreneurs are $100 for one year; for investors, $200 for three years.

Western Investment Network (WIN)

411 University Street
Suite 1200
Seattle, WA 98101
(206) 441-3123
FAX: (206) 463-6386
CONTACT: Steve Loyd
GEOGRAPHY: Pacific Northwest

WIN seeks to "create a more efficient market for entrepreneurs to introduce their business ventures to prospective business angels and strategic partners." WIN primarily serves ventures in Idaho, Oregon, Washington, and British Columbia. There are about 700 investors in WIN's database and 60 companies. Companies are usually seeking between $50,000 and $1 million in equity financing. WIN also requires that the companies have a business plan and transactional advisers. Annual fees are $100 for private investors and $650 for corporate investors; fees for entrepreneurs are $100 to submit a business plan and $650 for a six-month access to the network. The network claims to have a 20 percent success rate in matching entrepreneurs with investors.

SOURCES: Some of the entries listed in this directory were provided by KirkWorks, the National Recycling Coalition, and the U.S. Environmental Protection Agency (EPA); and excerpted from *A Financing Guide for Recycling Businesses: Investment Forums, Meetings and Networks*. This guide can be requested from the U.S. EPA RCRA hotline at (800) 424-9346, or accessed on the World Wide Web at www.epa.gov.

ADDITIONAL RESOURCES

DIRECTORIES AND MANUALS

- ◆ **The Ernst & Young Guide to Taking Your Company Public.** Authoritative and broad in its scope. Call John Wiley & Sons at 800-225-5945.
- ◆ **Direct Public Offerings.** This book was written by Drew Field, a securities attorney, certified public accountant (CPA), and DPO consultant. *Direct Public Offerings* provides a comprehensive step-by-step guide on taking your company public, as well as case studies of companies that underwent the DPO process. Call Sourcebooks, Inc. at 630-961-3900.
- ◆ **Galante's Venture Capital & Private Equity Directory.** Provides

comprehensive information on venture capital and buyout firms. *Galante's* comes with monthly updates of all the latest venture capital sources. Call Asset Alternatives, Inc. 781-431-7353.

◆ **Pratt's Guide to Venture Capital Sources.** *Pratt's Guide* is one of the most revered tomes, with almost 30 years' experience publishing on institutional venture capital sources. Current editions of *Pratt's Guide* provide detailed profiles on more than 1,200 institutional venture capital sources. Call Securities Data Company at 212-765-5311.

◆ **Regional Investment Banker's Membership Directory.** This trade-group membership directory provides detailed profiles on approximately 150 regional and boutique brokerage firms that concentrate on IPOs. Call the Regional Investment Bankers Association at 803-577-2000.

◆ **Self Directed IPO.** A two-volume set published by DataMerge, Inc., tells you everything you need to know about how to register and market a public offering using SCORs. Call DataMerge at 800-580-1188.

◆ **Partnerships: A Compendium of State and Federal Cooperative Technology Programs** is an exhaustive compilation of state and federal programs to assist technology-oriented companies. Many of the programs help companies with technology transfer, business planning, or industrial problem solving in addition to providing seed and grant financings. Contact Battelle Press, 505 King Avenue, Columbus, Ohio, 43201; 800-451-3543; or at **www.battelle.org/bookstore.**

PERIODICALS

◆ **Entrepreneur Magazine**. The magazine's "Raising Money" column is written by me and delivers sources and techniques on capital formation each month. Call (415) 261-2325. *See also* **www.entrepreneurmag.com.**

◆ **Going Public: The IPO Reporter.** *Going Public* is considered the bible of initial public offerings. The reputation is merited as *Going Public* is the only publication that provides enough data to evaluate IPO investment bankers from filing to aftermarket performance. At $950 per year, it's expensive, but worth it for companies dead serious about an IPO. Call (212) 227-1200.

◆ The **Private Equity Analyst**. This newsletter/journal is published monthly by former *Wall Street Journal* reporter Steven Galante. It provides fresh scuttlebutt on what's happening among venture capital firms, as well as the firms that invest in venture capital firms. *See also* **www.assetalt.com.**

◆ The **Red Herring**. A monthly publication that gives "an inside look at the latest deals and strategies in the digital universe." As a result, a lot of *Red Herring's* content, from ads to copy, covers venture capitalists, investment bankers, and the professionals who serve entrepreneurs. Call (415) 865-2277. *See also* **www.herring.com.**

◆ The **SCOR Report**. The only publication focusing exclusively on SCOR (Small Company Offering Registration) offerings. Call (972) 620-2489. **www.scor-report.com.**

◆ **Venture Capital Journal**. This monthly journal is primarily a trade magazine, but in the process provides good leads for venture capital investors. Call (212) 765-5311.

◆ **VentureEdge**. If you are looking for institutional capital, VentureEdge will tell you who is doing what on a quarterly basis. It is not cheap, however. The advertised price is $795. Call 415-538-2650. The publisher, VentureOne, offers a full range of products, including custom searches of its databases for likely venture capital investors. *See also* **www.ventureone.com.**

WEB SITES

◆ **https://:ace-net.sr.unh.edu/**. The "s" is in the address because Ace-Net is a secure site that limits where visitors can go. Still, it's worth a look and provides information available on how entrepreneurs and investors can utilize the Ace-Net initiative.

◆ **www.adventurecapital.com**. The Adventure site is essentially a fee-based matching service. The ancillary articles and information are good, however.

◆ **www.datamerge.com**. Provides forms for SCOR offerings, a financing-sources data bank, and product information on the firm's software product, which matches entrepreneurs and investors.

◆ **www.e-iponet.com**. This site bills itself as "the Internet site cleared by the SEC to sell public and private issues on-line." Worth a look.

◆ **www.ideacafe.com**. Despite the campy title, the "Financing Your Biz" hot button leads to useful lists and information for debt and equity financings.

◆ **www.ipocentral.com**. This site is primarily for investors, however it maintains a list of active IPO underwriters as well.

◆ **www.moneyhunter.com**. The alter ego of the Money Hunt television show that airs on 90 public television stations around the country. Provides valuable how-to and where-to-go-next information, including a business plan template.

◆ **www.moneysearch.com**. Strong on information about direct public offerings and SCOR offerings. Also offers several educational tools and links to IPO and venture capital–related sites. www.nasaa.org. This site is sponsored by the North American Securities Administrators Association and provides information on securities laws, plus initiatives to ease capital formation for small businesses.

◆ **www.sbaonline.sba.gov/inv/**. Explains the Small Business Investment Company (SBIC) program and provides links to some SBICs.

◆ **www.venturea.com**. The site's NetNews publishes a wide range of articles on venture capital financing and links to venture capital clubs.

Appendix B

UNIVERSITIES WITH LEADING ENTREPRENEURSHIP PROGRAMS

ALTHOUGH UNIVERSITIES WITH ENTREPRENEURSHIP PROGRAMS TEND to have a number of outreach programs to assist entrepreneurs, that is not the purpose of listing them here. According to Bob Tosterud, who heads the Council of Entrepreneurship Chairs, angel investors often hover around university-based entrepreneurship programs and have close ties with professors or other officials in the program. As a result, entrepreneurship programs can often provide formal or informal access to angel investors.

The following list of entrepreneurship programs was assembled from a variety of sources, including *Success* magazine's annual survey of the top 25 business schools, the membership of the Council of Entrepreneurship Chairs, and a paper titled "Measuring Progress in Entrepreneurship Education," by Karl Vesper and William Gartner, published in the *Journal of Business Venturing*. If you do not see a school near you, Tosterud suggests contacting *any* university nearby. "If there's an entrepreneurship program, it's worth your time to ask the person running it if they can help you."

◆ **Babson College**
F. W. Olin Graduate School of Business
Arthur M. Blank Center for Entrepreneurial Studies
Babson Park, MA
CONTACT: William Bygrave
781-239-4420

◆ **Ball State University**
College of Business
Midwest Entrepreneurial Education Center
Muncie, IN
CONTACT: Dr. Donald F. Kuratko
765-285-9002

◆ **University of Baltimore**
The Merrick School of Business
Center for Technology Commercialization
Baltimore, MD
CONTACT: Dr. Lanny Herron or Dr. Zoltan Acs
410-837-5012

◆ **Baylor University**
Hankamer School of Business
John F. Baugh Center for Entrepreneurship
Waco, TX

CONTACT: J. David Allen
254-710-2265

◆ **Beloit College**
Beloit, WI
CONTACT: Jerry Gustafson, Chairman
608-363-2343

◆ **University of California at Berkeley**
Haas School of Business
Lester Center for Entrepreneurship & Innovation
Berkeley, CA
CONTACT: Jerome S. Engel
510-642-1405

◆ **California State University, Fresno**
Sid Craig School of Business
Institute for Developing Entrepreneurial Action
Fresno, CA
CONTACT: Timothy M. Stearns
209-278-2482

◆ **University of California at Los Angeles**
Harold Price Center for Entrepreneurial Studies
The Anderson School at UCLA
Los Angeles, CA
CONTACT: Prof. Alfred E. Osborne, Jr.
310-825-2985

◆ **Carnegie Mellon University**
Graduate School of Industrial Administration
Donald H. Jones Center for Entrepreneurship
Pittsburgh, PA
CONTACT: Prof. John R. Thorne
412-268-2263

◆ **Case Western Reserve University**
Weatherhead School of Management
Cleveland, OH
CONTACT: Robert D. Hisrich
216-368-5354

◆ **University of Colorado**
College of Business
CU-Boulder Center for Entrepreneurship
Boulder, CO
CONTACT: G. Dale Meyer, or Denis B. Nock
303-492-5576

◆ **Cornell University**
Johnson Graduate School of Management
Ithaca, NY
CONTACT: David J. BenDaniel

607-255-4220

◆ **DePaul University**
Charles H.Kellstadt Graduate School of Business
Management Department
Chicago, IL
CONTACT: Harold P. Welsch
312-362-8364

◆ **Georgia State University**
Small Business Development Center
Atlanta, GA
CONTACT: Lee Quarterman
404-651-3550

◆ **University of Georgia**
Business Outreach Services/ Small Business Development Center
Athens, GA
CONTACT: Hank Logan
706-542-6762

◆ **Harvard Business School**
Graduate School of Business Administration
Boston, MA
CONTACT: Howard H. Stevenson
617-495-6339

◆ **University of Illinois at Chicago**
College of Business Administration
Institute for Entrepreneurial Studies
Chicago, IL
CONTACT: Gerald E. Hills
312-996-2670

◆ **Indiana University Research Park**
Kelley School of Business
Center for Entrepreneurship and Innovation
Bloomington, IN
CONTACT: Elizabeth Gatewood
812-855-4248

◆ **Kennesaw State University**
The Michael J. Coles School of Business
Kennesaw, GA
CONTACT: Timothy S. Mescon
770-423-6425

◆ **University of Louisville**
College of Business and Public Administration
Louisville, KY
CONTACT: Dr. Van G.H. Clouse
502-852-4782

◆ **University of Maryland**
   The Robert H. Smith School of Business
   Michael D. Dingman Center for Entrepreneurship
   College Park, MD
   CONTACT: Charles O. Heller
   301-405-2144

◆ **Miami University of Ohio**
   Richard T. Farmer School of Business Administration
   Thomas C. Page Center for Entrepreneurs
   Oxford, OH
   CONTACT: Dr. John W. Altman
   513-529-5409

◆ **University of Minnesota**
   Carlson School of Management
   Minneapolis, MN 55455
   CONTACT: Richard N. Cardozo
   612-624-5524

◆ **University of Nebraska-Lincoln**
   College of Business Administration
   The Nebraska Center for Entrepreneurship
   Lincoln, NE
   CONTACT: Dr. Terry Sebora
   402-472-3353

◆ **University of North Carolina-Chapel Hill**
   Kenan-Flagler Business School
   Center for Entrepreneurship and Technology Venturing
   Chapel Hill, NC
   CONTACT: Dr. Rollie Tillman or Jeff Reid
   919-962-2031

◆ **Northwestern University**
   J. L. Kellogg Graduate School of Management
   Heizer Center for Entrepreneurial Studies
   Evanston, IL
   Contact: Morton Kamien
   847-491-5167

◆ **University of the Pacific**
   Eberhardt School of Business
   Pacific Entrepreneurship Center
   Stockton, CA
   CONTACT: James O. Fiet
   209-946-3910

◆ **University of Pennsylvania, The Wharton School**
   Sol C. Snider Entrepreneurial Center
   Philadelphia, PA
   CONTACT: Ian MacMillan

215-898-4856

◆ **Rensselaer Polytechnic Institute**
Lally School of Management and Technology
Center for Technological Entrepreneurship
Troy, NY
CONTACT: William Stitt
518-276-8398

◆ **Saint Louis University**
School of Business & Administration
The Jefferson Smurfit Center for Entrepreneurial Studies
St. Louis, MO
CONTACT: Dr. Robert H. Brockhaus
314-977-2222

◆ **St. Mary's University, San Antonio**
School of Business & Administration
Algur H. Meadows Center for Entrepreneurial Studies
San Antonio, TX
CONTACT: Paul Goelz, S.M., Ph.D.
210-436-3124

◆ **University of St. Thomas**
Graduate School of Business
Center for Entrepreneurship
Minneapolis, MN
CONTACT: Nancy M. Carter or Cheryl Babcock
651-962-4400

◆ **San Diego State University**
The Entrepreneurial Management Center
San Diego, CA
CONTACT: Sanford B. Ehrlich, Ph.D.
619-594-2781

◆ **Sierra Nevada College**
Department of Business
Incline Village, NV
Contact: Dr. Gary Valiere
702-831-1314

◆ **University of South Dakota**
School of Business
Vermillion, SD
CONTACT: Robert J. Tosterud
605-677-5565

◆ **University of Southern California**
Marshall School of Business
Entrepreneur Program
Los Angeles, CA
CONTACT: Thomas J. O'Malia

213-740-3917

◆ **University of Tennessee, Chattanooga**
School of Business & Administration
Center for Economic Education
Chattanooga, TN
CONTACT: Dr. J.R. Clark
423-755-4118

◆ **University of Texas at Austin**
College & Graduate School of Business
Austin, TX
CONTACT: Dr. Gary M. Cadenhead
512-471-5289

◆ **Tulane University**
A. B. Freeman School of Business
Levy-Rosenblum Institute for Entrepreneurship
New Orleans, LA
CONTACT: Lina Alfieri Stern
504-865-5455

◆ **University of Tulsa**
College of Business Administration
Tulsa, OK
CONTACT: George S. Vozikis
918-631-3673

◆ **Wilkes University**
School of Business, Society, & Public Policy
Allan P. Kirby Center for Free Enterprise & Entrepreneurship
Wilkes-Barre, PA
CONTACT: Jeffrey Alves
717-408-4592

◆ **University of Wisconsin, Madison**
School of Business
Madison, WI
CONTACT: Prof. Jon G. Udell
608-263-4100

Appendix C
OVERVIEW OF SECURITIES LAWS INFLUENCING PRIVATE AND EXEMPT TRANSACTIONS

PROBABLY THE ONLY BARRIER STANDING BETWEEN INVESTORS AND the unbridled salesmanship of entrepreneurs is federal and state securities laws. The many layers of regulation are so complex that it is an act of courage to attempt discourse on securities laws without the benefit of a legal background. Chiefly this is because, without formal legal training, the remaining tool is common sense, which quickly becomes woefully inadequate in this arena.

Securities laws prove bewildering for several reasons. First, they exist both at the federal and state level. In addition to the Securities and Exchange Commission (SEC), which was created in the 1930s, every state in the nation fields its own securities commission, which, generally speaking, carries out its duties with vigor.

Second, they are antiquated. For instance, at the federal level, the Securities Act of 1933 dates back to a time when the nation was still reeling from the crash of 1929 and the word "Nasdaq" was a bluff in a Scrabble game.

Third, changes in capital formation are raising thorny policy questions that not even the regulators are certain how to address. If an entrepreneur in New York generates interest and eventually an investment through a private capital network from an investor in England, are federal and New York state securities laws invoked? Are any U.S. securities laws invoked?

Fourth, securities regulators are perhaps the most tenacious of all regulators. Of course, each new investment scam is more horrible than the one that preceded it and salvation lies in regulation; however, the application of these rules extracts a terrible burden upon upstanding corporate citizens.

This environment notwithstanding, entrepreneurs seeking to raise capital from private investors in more than one state may be exempt from registration under the Securities Act of 1933, a federal law that governs the public sale of securities (and which, incidentally, is a bear) by adhering to the rules set forth in f and Regulation A of the 1933 act.

REGULATION D

SO-CALLED REG D IS MADE OF UP SIX RULES. THE FIRST THREE OF these rules deal with definitions, general conditions, and disclosure requirements (i.e., what the company must tell investors), while the latter three deal with the kinds of offerings that are permitted under Regulation D. The following is a quick and essential overview of the definitions, as well as the kinds of offerings permitted by Reg D.

◆ **Definitions.** Eight terms are defined in Regulation D. Of these, the most important is the definition of an accredited investor. Of the 16 definitions of *accredited* investors, the most relevant is the one that applies to individuals, as opposed to institutions such as banks and insurance companies. An individual who is an accredited investor has a net worth or joint net worth with spouse in excess of $1 million at the time they are purchasing any securities; or they have net income in excess of $200,000 or joint income with spouse in excess of $300,000 in each of the last two years and they reasonably expect similar income in the current year.

◆ **Rule 504, offerings up to $1 million.** Rule 504 is the least restrictive of the exemptions and allows companies to raise $1 million in any 12-month period. There are no restrictions on the number or the qualifications of investors. Unlike other Regulation D rules, Rule 504 allows for advertising and solicitation of investors. Perhaps most important, under Rule 504, shares purchased by investors are freely transferable, without restriction placed on their resale.

◆ **Rule 505, offerings up to $5 million.** Offerings under Rule 505 may be sold to no more than 35 nonaccredited investors and/or an unlimited number of accredited investors. When nonaccredited investors are in the deal, certain information disclosure requirements about the offering and company come into play.

◆ **Rule 506, unlimited private offerings.** Under Rule 506, the same limitation on nonaccredited investors applies, but with one additional caveat. The issuer, that is, the company selling the securities, must "reasonably" believe that the nonaccredited investors have ample sophistication to evaluate the deal on its merits and understand the inherent risks and opportunities. And again, when nonaccredited investors are in the deal, certain information disclosure requirements materialize.

REGULATION A

SO-CALLED REG A OFFERS THE SAME EXEMPTION FROM REGISTRATION under the Securities Exchange Act of 1933 offered by Regulation D, but with important distinctions—some good, some restrictive. The good parts are that companies can issue up to $5 million in any 12-month period, there are no restrictions on the number or qualifications of the investors, and there are no restrictions on the resale of securities.

On the flip side, Regulation A may require that companies have positive net income and that an offering circular similar to a prospectus (in scope and degree of difficulty) be provided to investors. While the feds don't require audited financial statements in this circular, some states do. The circular, as part of a more comprehensive offering statement, must be filed with, reviewed, and cleared by the SEC. Uh-oh.

One frequently touted advantage that Regulation A enjoys over Regulation D is its "testing-the-waters" provision. This allows entrepreneurs to promote their offering through the media or live presentations prior to filing the SEC-required offering statement, and gauge whether sufficient interest exists in the deal to warrant the expense of moving forward.

Although this seems like a handy tool, in practice it's rarely used. Principally this is because most entrepreneurs assume there will be sufficient interest, while the attitude of high-strung intermediaries such as small brokerage firms that place the offering is that they are either doing a deal or they aren't. Finally, the testing-the-waters provision is rarely dusted off because it's difficult enough to solicit investors once; there's little to be gained, except more work, by trying to do it twice.

INTRASTATE OFFERINGS AND STATE SECURITIES LAWS

FINALLY, AS ANY DISCIPLE OF THE U.S. CONSTITUTION WOULD suspect, any intrastate offering—one that is sold to investors within the borders of a single state—is exempt from registration under the Securities Act of 1933, via the SEC's Rule 147. The reasoning goes that an offering within a state is that state's province, and that the imposition of any federal requirement constitutes a violation of its sovereignty. Accordingly, offerings that are exempt under Rule 147 need only meet the requirements of the relevant state's securities laws. However, along with selling only to residents of one state, those residents can't resell shares to out-of-state persons for nine months; at least 80 percent of the money raised has to be spent in that state (which has to be the "home" state of the business); and other strict rules. However, in many cases, the states are where the trouble can begin for entrepreneurs because state securities administrators often have very different views regarding the protection of investors in their domain.

For instance, while federal securities laws set simple standards regarding the disclosure of information to investors in a Regulation D offering, many so-called merit states actually set suitability standards that the company or the investors must meet to participate in an offering. And while the feds say it's okay to advertise a Reg D, Rule 504 offering and solicit investors, many state securities regulators say such activity is strictly verboten.

With 51 sets of regulators to contend with—50 states and one federal government—entrepreneurs face a myriad of inconsistencies, agendas, and intents. Sometimes these inconsistencies conspire to produce unusual, and at times, undesirable results. For instance, when Apple Computer went public, investors in Massachusetts could not purchase stock in the initial public offering (IPO), because the then tiny computer maker could not pass muster on the merit review. Apparently, there was some puritanical residue in the state's securities laws.

Worse, the problem can be compounded in an Internet-based matching environment such as the one Ace-Net is operating in, where the idea of a boundary is very difficult to control. To see this in action, consider the following hypothetical, but possible scenario:

An investor in one state could see an offering on Ace-Net for a company in Colorado. Even though the offering is not registered with the investor's state securities commission, he or she might nonetheless contact the entrepreneur. Further suppose that the investor visits the entrepreneur and a handshake deal is struck for the company to sell to the investor common shares in the company. To ensure the legality of the transaction, the entrepreneur then registers the offering in the investor's state. The regulators there declare the offering illegal and prevent its consummation. Why? Because the investor's state, like many others, has a prohibition against soliciting investors in the state without prior registration of the offering, and posting an advertisement of the deal on a national network visible to the state's investors constitutes such a solicitation. This doesn't mean that cooler heads won't prevail in the final analysis, but there's no guarantee they will either. After all, regulators exist to regulate.

At the state level, the best news is the growing popularity of the Small Company Offering Registration (SCOR)-form, also known as Form U-7. Basically, the SCOR form, which gave rise to the term "SCOR offerings," is a common registration statement accepted by every state except Alabama, Delaware, Hawaii, and Nebraska for offerings of less than $1 million.

Such offerings, because of their size, are also exempt from federal securities laws under Regulation D. Using a SCOR form, companies can easily file a registration statement for their offering in several states in which they want to sell the offering.

While filing of the registration statement is made easier by virtue of the SCOR form, gaining the separate approval of the states to sell the securities is another matter altogether. Some states provide a rubber stamp; others give entrepreneurs a hard time. In a favorable trend, the states have established regional review so that only one state in each region will actually go over the filing and make comments on behalf of all the others. This coordinated review is now available for Regulation A and other small-business filings.

Index

Detailed lists of organizations and other resources, not indexed here, are located in the following sections:

◆ **Appendix A:** *Directories and Manuals, Periodicals, Private Capital Networks, Private Equity Capital Directory, Venture Capital Clubs, and Web Sites.*

◆ **Appendix B:** *Universities with Leading Entrepreneurship Programs.*

A

C

M

273

N

279

About Bloomberg

Bloomberg Financial Markets is a global, multimedia-based distributor of information services, combining news, data, and analysis for financial markets and businesses. Bloomberg carries real-time pricing, data, history, analytics, and electronic communications that are available 24 hours a day and are currently accessed by 250,000 financial professionals in 94 countries.

Bloomberg covers all key global securities markets, including equities, money markets, currencies, municipals, corporate/euro/sovereign bonds, commodities, mortgage-backed securities, derivative products, and governments. The company also delivers access to Bloomberg News, whose more than 540 reporters and editors in 80 bureaus worldwide provide around-the-clock coverage of economic, financial, and political events.

To learn more about Bloomberg—one of the world's fastest-growing real-time financial information networks—call a sales representative at:

Frankfurt:	49-69-920-410
Hong Kong:	852-2521-3000
London:	44-171-330-7500
New York:	1-212-318-2000
Princeton:	1-609-279-3000
San Francisco:	1-415-912-2960
São Paulo:	5511-3048-4500
Singapore:	65-226-3000
Sydney:	61-29-777-8686
Tokyo:	81-3-3201-8900

About the Author

David R. Evanson is a principal and founder of Financial Communications Associates, Inc., an investor relations and consulting firm in Ardmore, Pennsylvania. Mr. Evanson has worked with a wide variety of public and private companies helping them find and communicate with institutional and individual investors. Mr. Evanson is an accomplished speaker and writer, and his work has appeared in *Forbes, Success, Nation's Business,* and *Venture* magazines, among others. His column, "Raising Money," is published monthly in *Entrepreneur* magazine. He resides in Swarthmore, Pennsylvania, with his wife, Perri, and two children, David and Madeline.

Readers with questions and comments can reach David Evanson by e-mail at devanson@aol.com or by mail at Financial Communications, 27 West Athens Avenue, Suite 200, Ardmore, PA 19003.